101 Tarot Spreads

By

Sheilaa Hite, C.Ht, C.L.C., C.P.C.

©2014

Temperance card cover art from The Gilded Tarot Royale Deck used by permission from the artist, Ciro Marchetti
ciromarchetti.com

Author's photo by Stephanie Stanton, www.stephaniestantonphotography.com

Published by The Center for Spiritual Practicality

Printed in the United States of America

ISBN 978-0-9916553-0-4

The Center for Practical Spirituality
P.O. Box 472
Lenox, MA 01240 USA

www.SheilaaHite.com

Also by Sheilaa Hite

The Spiritual Hedonist—a Guide to the Divine Art of Living Joyfully

The Infinite Tarot

Secrets of a Psychic Counselor

Power Secrets

Contents

SPREADS—

Romantic Relationships

Platonic Relationships

Prosperity, Creativity and Goals

Know Thyself

Cycles and Assessments

Past Lives and Karma

Choices and Options

Personal Growth

General Spreads

I dedicate this book to
my teachers and students-- past, present and future

✑

Acknowledgements

"Let us be grateful to the people who make us happy;
they are the charming gardeners who make our souls blossom."
Marcel Proust

As always, the birthing of any creative venture requires many people to bring it about. The making of 101 Tarot Spreads is no different. And, as always, thankfully, the Divine spark from the "Front Office" inspired and encouraged me to write this book.

A heartfelt and soul deep expression of gratitude to the incredibly gifted artist, Ciro Marchetti for allowing me to use the Temperance card from his Gilded Tarot ROYALE deck and to Tarot treasure, Mary K. Greer, Magpie Oracle creator, Carrie Paris and Tarot aficionado, Paris Finley for valuing my work and having faith in me.

To earth angel, Siobhan Kleinman who sought me out and delivered the "Front Office's" message to me—"You need to go to the next Readers Studio Tarot conference." Knowing a Divine mandate when I hear one, I went and the course of my life changed—thank you so much!

I am eternally grateful for the support of my students and friends in my Advanced Tarot workshop—Winslow Eliot, Ginny Guenette, Louise Rossi-Edwards, Ralston Edwards, Dawn Danis, Janet Jendrzejewski, Billie Chernicoff, Meghna Bhagat, Dr. Janice Seward, Teresa Clancy, Linda Farmer and Robin Hare. In addition to being the positive, encouraging, generous mirrors of my value and commitment to fully engage with life, they were also willing to 'test drive' these spreads, critique my work and give me positive feedback.

A special thanks to Linda Farmer, Winslow Eliot, Ginny Guenette, Louise Rossi-Edwards, Ralston Edwards, David Nathan and Jennifer Lamb for allowing me to include their wonderfully insightful spreads in this collection.

Many hugs to Linda Farmer for designing the format of the spreads in this book and for teaching me how to use it and to Winslow Eliot and Tom Stier for their wisdom and generosity as they edited and published the manuscript.

An infinite amount of thanks to the phenomenal Tim Moriarty and his immensely talented graphic artist, Gleb Jerebtsov at Square One Design for working their magic and beautifully 'channeling' my cover concept into physical reality. And a very appreciative 'Thank You!' to the wonderfully gifted Angela Flores of Paisley Prints, Etc. for making my text and Tarot spreads look great.

I thank God every day that I have such loving, encouraging dear friends as David Nathan, James Wecker of DearJames™, Joanne and Al Abney and Doreene Hamilton for believing in me and for insisting on only the best for and from me.

Again and forever, I thank my guardian angel, my maternal grandmother, Lois, with all my heart. I love you and thank you for helping me to see myself as being as beautiful as you see me. With illimitable love, I thank you for watching over me, I feel your love and your wings around me always.

Introduction

*"The educator must believe in the potential power of his pupil,
and he must employ all his art in seeking to bring his pupil to experience this power."*
Alfred Adler

Tarot cards and Tarot spreads are part of a record keeping GPS system that can help guide you in answering important questions and making your dreams come true. In order to find value in the guidance, it must be delivered through the system in such a way that it provides the answers to your questions and the instructions for attaining your goals.

101 Tarot Spreads is a rich and varied collection of maps—some light and whimsical, some profound and intense, some mundane and practical and some eclectic and conceptual. The purpose of this collection of Tarot spreads is to give you a clearer, more powerful way of accessing the vital information that is important to you and your well-being as you continue to live and evolve.

By using the spreads in this book, your relationship with the Tarot will become a personal, intuitive one in which the cards speak to you. As you learn to listen to them and trust what they tell you through the device of the Tarot spreads, you'll appreciate how well they help you find your way. In the process of learning to establish a relationship with the cards and with the spreads, you'll learn so much more about yourself, others and life.

I was born with the gift of active intuition and as an Intuitive Counselor, I've learned that I can clearly see all aspects of my client's issues and find previously hidden solutions to their most vexing problems. As a teacher, I've learned that I can show others how to find and develop their own very accurate, powerful relationship with the Tarot and themselves.

Because of my intuitive relationship with the Tarot, my accuracy rate is 95-100% and I've been told by clients and students alike, that my ability to interpret the cards is legendary.

A natural detective, I'm an expert at looking for and finding the solution to whatever quandary that presents itself to me. Because I didn't get my initial intuitive or Tarot training from books or

1

corporeal teachers, I didn't learn that certain energy, suits, elements, cards or spreads are considered 'bad', 'weak', 'good' or 'strong'. I learned to accept all of them, to observe them and to listen to them as they presented themselves to me at the time that a question is asked or an issue is raised. I learned that they'll always organically reflect the energy of the seeker, the situation and the question.

Because I learned this way, and because it works, I interpret and I teach this way. My students find and nurture their own inner greatness just as I did with my Guides. They better understand themselves, life and the Tarot through becoming conscious of their own mastery as they study with me.

And that is what I offer you in 101 Tarot Spreads, an opportunity to view the world in a new, more empowered way. Through using the spreads in this book, you will discover infinite opportunities to encounter and develop a deeper, more intuitive relationship with the Tarot and yourself.

What is a Tarot Spread?

A good Tarot spread is a priceless ally. When cards are laid out in a spread, a story line with themes, meanings and characters is revealed. The weaving of this story and the perspective gained from it are essential to the art of accurate interpretation.

An accurate Tarot reading helps to solve the mysteries of life, and as with all mysteries, it's the clues and the interpretation of those clues that are the keys to getting your answers.

The Tarot cards are the clues that provide the answers; the Tarot spreads are the maps that tell you what story is being told and how to accurately read the clues that will reveal the most direct path to the answers to your questions. Like all good maps, a good Tarot spread shows you where you are, how you got there, what the topography is like, and how to get to where you want to go.

In this book, you'll find all kinds of Tarot spreads that will help guide you in your quest for the answers to your questions about life—relationships, security, spirituality and all of the areas in between.

As you work with the Tarot spreads in this book, you may feel the need to make your own changes to them or use them for different subjects or issues, please feel free to do so. As I've said many times before, the Intuitive Arts and its processes are part of an experiential realm, as you progress and adapt to them, they must, in turn, adapt to you. It's a good idea to make copies of the original spreads for future use.

What Can the Tarot Be Used For?

You can use the Tarot to enlighten yourself about all manner of subjects, from the loftiest of matters to the most mundane of issues. The Tarot is an information retrieval system, whose purpose is to help you get the information you're seeking.

You can use the oracle for anything as mundane as choosing which movie you're going to see to something as ethereal as communicating with your guardian angels.

The Tarot is a powerful tool; the definition of tool is "a device or implement used to carry out a particular function." It's an aid meant to help you better understand yourself, your world and the people in it. You decide how you want to interact with and use this tool.

I use and interact with the Tarot in many, many ways. Some of them are:

1. As a mirror-- to follow the dictum carved on ancient Greek temples, "Know Thyself." I ask it questions that will reveal to me a better and deeper understanding of myself, my motives, my path, my purpose.
2. As confirmation-- often I've already come to a conclusion about something when I consult the cards and I want additional information.
3. As a tie breaker-- to help me decide between two or more courses of action, processes, routes, movies, events, purchases, etc.
4. As a sleuth-- to help me find the answers to the great mysteries of life, including, where I left my car keys.
5. As inspiration-- to help me connect with my creative center.
6. As a meditation guide-- to focus on the card pulled and 'follow' its lead as I meditate on the message its bringing me.
7. To connect to Spirit-- need I say more?
8. As a dear friend whom I know will always tell me the truth, whether I want to hear it or not.

How to Use the Major Arcana & Minor Arcana

"Arcana" is Latin for secrets. The Tarot deck consists of 78 cards divided into two main groups—the Major Arcana, meaning large or big secrets, which consists of 22 cards and the Minor Arcana, meaning small or personal secrets, consisting of 56 cards.

Each of the 78 Tarot cards in the deck reflects a pattern that is universal in all peoples in all cultures at all periods of history. Therefore, each card brings to your conscious mind a personal image that you relate to and can relate to the question or issue you are consulting the cards about. The Tarot acts as a mirror to the subconscious and reveals and reflects hidden knowledge related to the querent, question, issue or energy of the moment.

The 22 cards of the Major Arcana represent the stages of life or the processes we all go through in our lives. As we experience each of these stages or processes, we are given an opportunity to live and grow.

The Major Arcana represents the psychological over-view, the perspective of God or the gods, a higher authority and/or something outside our immediate control.

In many of the spreads in this book, you'll notice that I've designated certain positions in the spread to be interpreted with a Major Arcana card. That's because you'll get a clearer understanding that the information in that particular position often comes from a higher, more all-knowing and/or Divine source. For the spreads that call for it, separate the Major Arcana cards from the Minor Arcana and choose the Major Arcana cards for the specified positions first. Then shuffle both Arcanas together and pick the remaining cards from the deck unless otherwise instructed.

The 56 cards of the Minor Arcana represent life, life's experiences and our power or control in it. Representing our "hands-on" input in our experiences and how we personally deal with what we create or encounter in life, the Minor Arcana details the journey we all take in a more personal manner than the Major Arcana.

You'll notice that I've designated certain positions in the spread to be interpreted with a Minor Arcana card. Because the Minor Arcana represents our personal input in life, these are the positions where you'll have the opportunity to see what you're doing, have done or can do in the situation. For the spreads that call for it, separate the Minor Arcana cards from the Major Arcana and choose the Minor and Major Arcana cards for the specified positions. Then shuffle both Arcanas together and pick the remaining cards from the deck unless otherwise instructed.

The Minor Arcana is also divided into four suits of 14 cards each. Each suit represents the energy of a different element and expresses a particular area of life in specific detail from the perspective of the suit:

- Wands, the element of Fire
- Cups, the element of Water
- Swords, the element of Air
- Pentacles, the element of Earth

A Very Important Reminder on Gender and Court Cards

The terms "Masculine" and "Feminine" do not refer to gender. They refer, instead, to types of energy, and/or action and/or how an action takes place. The Feminine aspect is the Creative, the Generator, it feels, creates and wants. The Masculine aspect is the Activator, the Procurer, it thinks, plans and gets. Having a need or desire is Feminine; satisfying that need or desire is Masculine. They sometimes (though not always) represent actual people.

Court cards represent types of energy and character types. They DO NOT describe qualities limited to just men or women, they emphasize the active and receptive qualities of energy available to both women and men.

Clarifying Cards

A clarifying card is a card that is pulled to help you better understand an individual card in the spread or the entire spread. They can shed more light on the card, the querent, the issue and/or the spread.

Please don't over-do it, though. At the most, two or three clarifying cards are enough to help you decipher the clues in the other cards. Any more cards than that and you're right back in muddled confusion.

If the clarifying cards aren't helping you to clarify the message, you probably need to re-think the question and approach the answer from a different perspective.

Choosing your Tarot Deck

It goes without saying that if you're reading this book, you've probably already got at least one Tarot deck. Using that one deck will definitely give you access to great information. However, by only using that one deck, you can find yourself with a limited (and sometimes skewed) view of that information. Having access to more than one deck gives you the opportunity to have a more expansive view of the question, issue or person you're asking about, as well as the answers.

Sometimes, card readers feel they're being 'unfaithful' to their one and only Tarot deck if they start using a new deck. They shouldn't fret, though. Tarot decks are amazingly tolerant and won't be the least bit jealous if you bring a new deck into the 'family.' I currently work with seven Tarot decks. I let them 'tell' me which ones are to be used during a reading. (They 'tell' me energetically. I set them on a table and slowly move my right hand a few inches above them until I feel a strong energy pull to the correct deck.)

The Tarot works with you on an intuitive level, always seeking the depths of your infinite repository of knowledge. Being able to hear and allow yourself to listen to your inner voice via a different deck is a marvelous gift to give yourself and your clients. Embracing a new 'vehicle,' your new deck, which will transport you to your repository, is a deeply rewarding requisite for aligning your spirit with the Source of Knowledge.

The most important things to keep in mind when you choose any deck are, 1- "Does it appeal to me visually?" and 2- "How do I feel when I hold it in my hands?"

We're a visual species and the Tarot is a set of images and symbols that we first consciously encounter with our eyes. If you don't like the way a deck looks, don't bother with how it'll feel when you hold it. If you do like the way it looks, hold it in your right hand, bring it up to your chest and hold it over your heart. Close your eyes and take several deep, rhythmic, gentle breaths. And notice how you feel when you to that. Do you feel at peace, agitated, happy, sad? Is your heart calm or is it racing? What thoughts are going through your mind?

If you feel agitated or sad or you feel nothing at all, you're obviously not holding the deck that's meant for you. If your heart is racing, is it from excitement or trepidation? If it's from trepidation—that isn't your deck, either. If negative or self-deprecating thoughts are going through your mind, that's what working with that particular deck will bring you, put it back on the shelf.

If you feel at peace, calm, happy and/or positive thoughts are going through your mind, you've found your new Tarot deck. This clear indication that the two of you are ready for (to paraphrase the last line in the classic film, Casablanca), "The beginning of a beautiful friendship," is all the confirmation you'll need that you've made a good choice.

Special Bonus Charts

My Tarot Cards for the Month and Day

Month & Year: _____   Card: _____

	SUNDAY	MONDAY	TUESDAY	WEDNESDAY	THURSDAY	FRIDAY	SATURDAY
Week 1							
Week 2							
Week 3							
Week 4							
Week 5							

Observations:

How to Determine Your Life Path Number
and Major Arcana Life Path Card

My Life Path Number Is _____   *My Life Path Tarot Card Is:* _____

The month I was born (in numbers)_____

The date I was born _____

The year I was born (all 4 numbers) _____

Equals_____

Now add each number from the above total _____ + _____ + _____ + _____ = _____

If you get a double digit number, add those _____ + _____ = _____

The resulting single digit is your Life Path number. The Major Arcana Tarot card that matches your Life Path number is your Life Path card.

Example:

The month I was born (in numbers)	4
The date I was born	7
The year I was born (all 4 numbers)	1985
Equals	1996

Now add each number together from the above total: **1 + 9 + 9 + 6 = 25**

If you get a double digit number, add those **2 + 5 = 7**

My Life Path Number Is 7
My Life Path Tarot Card Is: **The Chariot**

My Major Arcana Tarot Card Teachers Chart

Make copies of the My Major Arcana Tarot Card Teachers for the Year form for future use. Each year, record your Major Arcana Teachers cards on it.

Separate the Major Arcana cards from the Minor Arcana cards and put the Minor Arcana cards off to the side, you won't be using them in this exercise. Remember, always count the Major Arcana cards to make sure you have all 22 in one stack.

Shuffle the Major Arcana cards and place them face down on a table in three rows. With your left hand, pick the card that represents your spiritual or inner lessons teacher for the year. Don't turn it over, yet. Set it to the side and with your right hand, pick the card that represents your worldly or outer lessons teacher for the year.

Now, turn both cards over and record the cards and your impressions of them on the form.

MY MAJOR ARCANA TAROT CARD TEACHERS FOR 20___

My Spiritual/Inner Teacher is Represented By _____

I Feel My Major Spiritual Lesson This Year Is—

****

My Worldly/Outer Teacher Is Represented By _____

I Feel My Major Worldly Lesson This Year Is—

****

I Feel My Combined Spiritual and Worldly Lessons This Year Can Teach Me—

Guided Tarot Meditations

Guided meditations are great for helping you access your inner consciousness. My guided meditations will help you establish and maintain a relationship with the cards, characters and information sources of the Tarot.

With the purchase of The Infinite Tarot guide, you also receive access to a free download of two of my Tarot guided meditations. Just go to my website—www.SheilaaHite.com and click on 'Store' and scroll down to 'Free Tarot Meditations Download' and click on that.

Recommended Books & Sources

The Infinite Tarot by Sheilaa Hite

Tarot For Yourself Workbook by Mary K. Greer

Mythology by Edith Anderson or *Bullfinch's Mythology* by Bullfinch

How to Read a Person like a Book by Gerald Nierenberg and Henry Calero

Numerology (any small volume will do)

A Thesaurus (synonyms & antonyms of words)

A book on colors and their meanings (any small volume will do)

The Alchemist by Paulo Coelho

The 1998 film, *The Red Violin* (superb Tarot tale!)

Tarot by Paris - **www.TarotbyParis.com**, antique, out of print, rare & modern Tarot decks, Tarot books, Astrology books

Tarot Garden - **www.tarotgarden.com**, antique, out of print, rare & modern Tarot decks

Malibu Shaman Bookstore – 23410 Civic Center Way, #E-5, Malibu, CA 90265
310-465-5617 – **www.malibushaman.com**, books, crystals, candles, gifts, music

Namaste Bookshop - 2 W. 14th St, New York, NY 10011 – 212- 645-0141
www.namastebookshop.com, books, crystals, candles, gifts, music

Romantic Relationships

"What the heart has once owned, it shall never lose."
Henry Ward Beecher

1- Are You 'The One'?

The **Are You 'The One'?** spread answers three of the most important questions to ask yourself before you commit to being in a serious relationship with someone:

- *Do they love you?*—do they feel a heart connection to you
- *Do they like you?*—are they your friend
- *Do they 'get' you?*—do they accept those unique (and sometimes vexing) qualities that come with being who you are.

Are You 'The One'?

Question

Feelings or Interpretation

Name
Date
Time
Deck

1) Do they like you?

2) Do they love you?

3) Do they 'get' you?

4) Their ability to commit

5) Their ability to compromise

6) Are the 2 of you compatible?

7) Their level of emotional maturity

8) Are you on the same Spiritual Path?

9) What you need to be aware of

Created by Sheilaa Hite

2- Is It Attraction, Infatuation or True Love?

The **Is It Attraction, Infatuation or True Love?** spread will help you sort out your real feelings for someone you are drawn to.

Is It Attraction, Infatuation or True Love?

Question   Name
                                                  Date
                                                  Time
Feelings or Interpretation   Deck

1) Attraction	1) Infatuation	1) True love
2) Attraction	2) Infatuation	2) True love
3) Attraction	3) Infatuation	3) True love

Inspired by Sheilaa Hite

3- Romantic Heart Spread

The **Romantic Heart Spread** examines the two of you as a couple from the perspective of the Universe and advises on the action required to attract and/or be in a healthy romantic relationship. It helps sort out and deal with the issues that surround a relationship and a current or potential significant other.

Romantic Heart Spread

Question

Feelings or Interpretation

Name
Date
Time
Deck

4)
How the
Universe sees me

2)
Major Arcana

The two of us as a
couple

7)
How the
Universe sees the
other person

5)
What the
Universe wants
me to know
regarding my
relationship
issues

1)
Major Arcana

Heart
of the Matter

8)
What the Universe
wants me to know
about the other
person regarding
their
relationship
issues

6)
Action I need to
take to attract
&/or be in a
healthy romantic
relationship

3)
Major Arcana

Main thing to
keep in mind
regarding this
relationship

9)
Action the other
person needs to
take to attract
&/or be in a
healthy
romantic
relationship

Created by Sheilaa Hite

4- Why Did This Relationship End?

The **Why Did This Relationship End?** spread is great for figuring out just what happened and how to let go.

Why Did This Relationship End?

Question   Name
                                                                                        Date
                                                                                        Time
Feelings or Interpretation   Deck

1)
What was the
purpose of this
relationship?

4)
Is it truly over?

2)
What was the
'last straw' that
ended it?

7)
What I've
learned from this
experience

5)
Why is it so
difficult to
let go of it?

3)
Could it ever
have worked out
in the long term?

6)
Action required
to move on

Created by Sheilaa Hite

5- Twin Flame Spread

The **Twin Flame Spread** will show you what is unique about your deep karmic relationship as well as the Divine intention for the relationship.

Twin Flame Spread

Question   Name
                                                           Date
                                                           Time
Feelings or Interpretation   Deck

1)
What unites us

2)
What is unique
about us

3)
What separates
us

4)
What holds us
together

5)
Who we are
together

6)
How we reflect
Divine intention

Created by Sheilaa Hite

6- Relationship Spread

The **Relationship Spread**. I don't have to tell you what this one's about. Everyone is interested in relationships—romantic, platonic, professional, familial. Use this spread to answer those age-old questions.

Relationship Spread

Question

Feelings or Interpretation

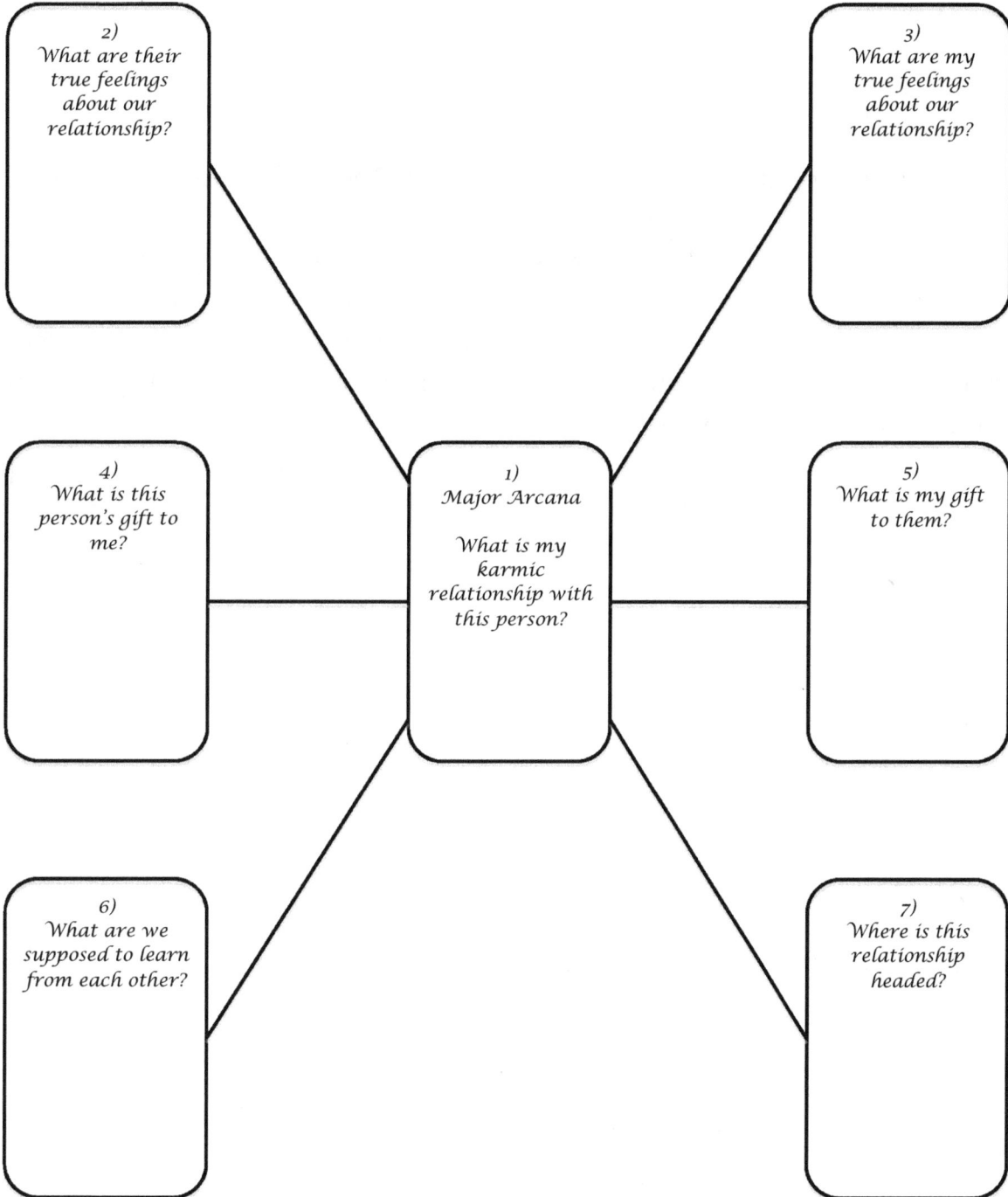

Name
Date
Time
Deck

2) What are their true feelings about our relationship?

3) What are my true feelings about our relationship?

4) What is this person's gift to me?

1) Major Arcana

What is my karmic relationship with this person?

5) What is my gift to them?

6) What are we supposed to learn from each other?

7) Where is this relationship headed?

Created by Sheilaa Hite

7- Date-O-Rama—How to Stop Being a Doormat in Relationships

The **Date-O-Rama—How to Stop Being a Doormat in Relationships** spread. Almost everyone has had an experience of being a doormat in a relationship. Knowing what motivates you to accept those less than ideal terms is the key to taking your power back and ending that negative cycle forever. This is a good spread for understanding all types of relationships—romantic, platonic or professional.

Date-O-Rama
How to Stop Being a Doormat in Relationships

Question

Name
Date
Time

Feelings or Interpretation

Deck

3)
True nature of
the problem

2)
Your greatest
relationship fear

6)
Major Arcana

You, the querent
and/or the heart
of the matter

4)
What you need to
do to take your
power back

1)
Your biggest
obstacle

5)
Your greatest
strengths

8- What I Need to Know About Myself in Relationships

The **What I Need to Know About Myself in Relationships** spread. The title says it all and the answers you get will help you to be in better relationship with yourself as well as a significant other. This is a good spread for understanding all types of relationships—romantic, platonic or professional.

What I Need to Know About Myself in Relationships

Question   Name
                                            Date
                                            Time
Feelings or Interpretation   Deck

1)
Am I available
for relationship
now?

3)
What I like
about being in
a relationship

2)
Am I ready for
relationship
now?

4)
What I dislike
about being in a
relationship

6)
What I think I
want in a
relationship

5)
What I fear
about being in
a relationship

7)
What I really
want in a
relationship

9)
Querent
and/or Heart
of the Matter

8)
How I resolve
and heal my
relationship
issues

Created by Sheilaa Hite

9- Is That All There Is?—Is This Relationship Worth Saving?

The **Is That All There Is?—Is This Relationship Worth Saving?** spread is an honest, in-your-face look at the relationship that's slipping away from you. Is it worth the effort to hold it together or is it better to let it go and move on? This is a good spread for understanding all types of relationships—romantic, platonic or professional.

Is That All There Is?
Is This Relationship Worth Saving?

Question

Name
Date
Time
Deck

Feelings or Interpretation

1)
Their true level
of interest

5)
How we are
compatible

2)
My true level
of interest

6)
How we are not
compatible

9)
The true nature of
this relationship

3)
What am I
refusing to see

7)
What forces are
helping us

4)
What am I
willing to admit

8)
What forces are
blocking us

Created by Sheilaa Hite

10- The Diamond Spread

The **Diamond Spread** helps you to know what your relationship is really about. It identifies and explains each party's motivation for being in the relationship.

The Diamond Spread

Question Is She/He My True Mate?

Feelings or Interpretation

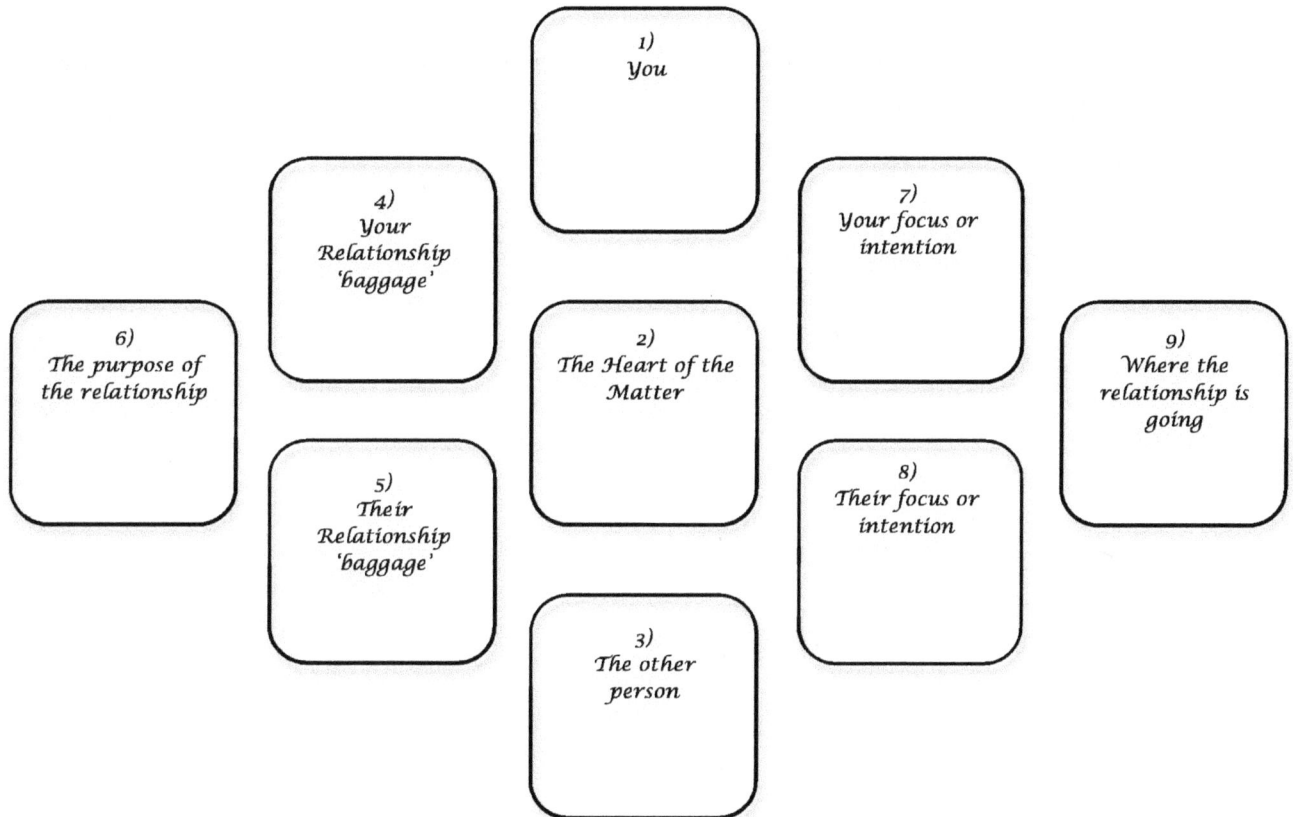

Name
Date
Time
Deck

1)
You

4)
Your
Relationship
'baggage'

7)
Your focus or
intention

6)
The purpose of
the relationship

2)
The Heart of the
Matter

9)
Where the
relationship is
going

5)
Their
Relationship
'baggage'

8)
Their focus or
intention

3)
The other
person

Created by Sheilaa Hite

11- The Queen's Cup

The Queen's Cup spread reminds me of the cup that the Queen of Cups holds in the Rider-Waite-Smith deck. It answers the very important question, *"Can this romantic involvement fulfill my relationship needs?"*

The Queen's Cup

Question

Feelings or Interpretation

Name
Date
Time
Deck

7) What other person needs to be aware of

11) What I need to be aware of

1) How the relationship appears to us

5) Other person's conscious relationship needs

9) My conscious relationship needs

8) What other person truly needs

12) What I truly need

2) How the relationship really is

6) Other person's subconscious relationship needs

10) My subconscious relationship needs

3) Advantages & disadvantages of this relationship

4) Action required regarding this relationship

Created by Sheilaa Hite

12- Why Do I Attract Dysfunctional Relationships?

The **Why Do I Attract Dysfunctional Relationships?** spread will help you understand the reasons for and change old self-defeating behaviors that cause you to be involved in dysfunctional relationships of all types—romantic, platonic and professional.

Why Do I Attract Dysfunctional Relationships?

Question

Feelings or Interpretation

Name
Date
Time
Deck

1)
What am I attracting?

2)
What do I really want?

3)
Why do I de-value myself?

4)
What do I need to heal?

5)
Action required to heal this issue

6)
What is my innate strength with this issue?

7)
Querent and/or Heart of the Matter

13- Two of Cups Spread

The **Two of Cups Spread** is great for assessing the type of relationship and the potential for success or failure at the very beginning. Often, the more you know and the earlier you know it can save you a lot of time, energy and angst. If the 2 of Cups appears in this spread, especially in the #1 position, it indicates the powerful potential for a deep soul connection.

Two of Cups Spread

Question   Name
                                                  Date
                                                  Time
Feelings or Interpretation   Deck

3)
Your conscious
responsibility
regarding this
relationship

2)
Physical
circumstances of
this relationship

6)
Major Arcana

The Heart of the
matter

4)
Spiritual lesson
of this
relationship

1)
Message from the
Universe
regarding this
relationship

5)
Action required
regarding this
relationship

Created by Sheilaa Hite

Platonic Relationships

"Each friend represents a world in us, a world possibly not born until they arrive,
and it is only by this meeting that a new world is born."
Anaïs Nin

14- My BFF—Friendship Spread

The **My BFF—Friendship Spread**. A BFF is a wonderful friend to have, but sometimes the relationship can be detrimentally imbalanced. This spread will help you to know whether you're standing on solid friendship ground or not.

My BFF—Friendship Spread

Question

Name
Date
Time
Deck

Feelings or Interpretation

3)
How I perceive
this friendship

2)
Is this friendship
balanced?

7)
The true gift of
this relationship

4)
How my BFF
perceives it

1)
Is this friendship
beneficial to me?

6)
Important thing
to remember
about our
friendship

5)
How the
Universe
perceives it

Created by Sheilaa Hite

15- In It for the Money—Business Partnership

The **In It for the Money—Business Partnership** spread is great for knowing who you, your time, energy, dreams and money are 'dancing' with.

In It for the Money—Business Partnership

Question

Feelings or Interpretation

Name
Date
Time
Deck

3)
Advantages of
this partnership

4)
Disadvantages of
this partnership

2)
Who am I?

5)
How will this
partnership
affect me?

1)
Who are they?

6)
Probability of
our success

8)
The bottom line

7)
What I'm not
aware of

Created by Sheilaa Hite

16- The Big Picture—for Groups, Projects and Humanitarian Pursuits

The Big Picture—for Groups, Projects and Humanitarian Pursuits spread will help you enjoy the success of making a difference in the world. It'll save you time, effort and disappointment if you pay attention to the information this spread gives you.

The Big Picture
For Groups, Projects and Humanitarian Pursuits

Question

Feelings or Interpretation

Name
Date
Time
Deck

6)
The strengths of the group, project or pursuit

1)
The group, project or pursuit

7)
The weaknesses of the group, project or pursuit

8)
Major Arcana

How to best use those strengths

2)
The intent of the group, project or pursuit

9)
Major Arcana

How to best overcome those weaknesses

10)
What radical shift of perspective will serve the purpose of the group, project or pursuit

3)
Major Arcana

Heart of the matter

11)
What progressive actions will serve the purpose of the group, project or pursuit

4)
Who/what opposes the group, project or pursuit

5)
Who/what supports the group, project or pursuit

Created by Sheilaa Hite's Tarot Circle Group

17- Conflict Resolution Spread

The **Conflict Resolution Spread** simply, effectively and powerfully puts it all out there so that you can take the wise, informed, positive action required to properly settle any conflict. It works well for individuals and counselors using it to help couples resolve their differences.

Conflict Resolution Spread

Question   Name
                                                  Date
                                                  Time
Feelings or Interpretation   Deck

1)
What I want

2)
What other
party wants

3)
What I don't like
but must accept

4)
What they don't
like but must
accept

5)
What is best for
all parties

Created by Sheilaa Hite

Prosperity, Creativity and Goals

"I have an idea; God has a plan."
Sheilaa Hite

.

18- Money Bags

The **Money Bags** spread is a great manifesting spread. Once you get a clear picture of what you need to do to activate and access your abundance in the ethereal realm, you'll be able to create it in the material realm.

Money Bags

Question

Feelings or Interpretation

Name
Date
Time
Deck

3 Seeds – What's needed to
activate your bounty

Major Arcana

What you can do to access your bounty

Major Arcana

Gold Nugget - What is hidden but was always there & will enhance and enrich the 3 Gifts

Major Arcana

3 Gifts - They are always paying dividends to you

Created by Sheilaa Hite

19- The Wish Spread

The Wish Spread is wonderful. It clearly shows you what your wish really means to you and how to make it come true.

***If the 9 of Cups appears in any position besides #'s 9, 10 and 11, it's a strong indicator that your wish will come true.

The Wish Spread

Question

Feelings or Interpretation

Name
Date
Time
Deck

3) Factors describing your wish **Cards 3, 4 & 5**	4) Factors describing your wish **Cards 3, 4 & 5**	5) Factors describing your wish **Cards 3, 4 & 5**
6) Who/what assists you **Cards 6, 7 & 8**	7) Who/what assists you **Cards 6, 7 & 8**	8) Who/what assists you **Cards 6, 7 & 8**

1) Querent	2) The Wish

9) Who/what opposes you **Cards 9, 10 & 11**	10) Who/what opposes you **Cards 9, 10 & 11**	11) Who/what opposes you **Cards 9, 10 & 11**
12) Action required on your part to make wish come true **Cards 12, 13 & 14**	13) Action required on your part to make wish come true **Cards 12, 13 & 14**	14) Action required on your part to make wish come true **Cards 12, 13 & 14**

Created by Sheilaa Hite

20- 'Tis Better to Receive...

The '**Tis Better to Receive...** spread will help dispel those old, negative belief systems that keep you from getting what you want.

'Tis Better to Receive...

Question

Feelings or Interpretation

Name
Date
Time
Deck

1)
Unconscious
expression of my
beliefs on
receiving/
having what I
want

2a)
How those
unconscious
beliefs serve or
inhibit me

2)
How those
unconscious
beliefs manifest
in my world

3)
Major Arcana

Heart of the
matter

4)
New perspective
on having what I
want or need

4a)
How this new
perspective on
having what I
want or need
serves me

5)
Major Arcana

My life lesson on
allowing myself
to receive

Created by Sheilaa Hite

21- Prosperity Spread

The **Prosperity Spread** is another powerfully dynamic tool that can help you access and resolve the issues pertaining to money, abundance, self-value and manifesting and accepting what you want and deserve to have.

Prosperity Spread

Question

Name
Date
Time
Deck

Feelings or Interpretation

2)
Major Arcana

What scarcity
means to me

3)
Major Arcana

What prosperity
means to me

7)
Minor Arcana
Cards 7, 8 & 9
What is blocking
me from
receiving my
prosperity

10)
Minor Arcana
Cards 10, 11 &
12
What will allow
me to accept my
prosperity

1)
Major Arcana

How the
Universe
provides for me

8)
Minor Arcana
Cards 7, 8 & 9
What is blocking
me from
receiving my
prosperity

11)
Minor Arcana
Cards 10, 11 &
12
What will allow
me to accept my
prosperity

4)
Major Arcana

Root cause of
positions 1, 2 & 3

9)
Minor Arcana
Cards 7, 8 & 9
What is blocking
me from
receiving my
prosperity

12)
Minor Arcana
Cards 10, 11 &
12
What will allow
me to accept my
prosperity

5)
Minor Arcana

What I think I
want

6)
Minor Arcana

What I really
want

22- The Magician Spread

The Magician Spread powerfully allows you to experience all of the magical aspects that go into creating what you want and bringing it to fruition in the material world.

The Magician Spread

Question

Feelings or Interpretation

Name
Date
Time
Deck

1)
Major Arcana

What streams
from the
Universe

2)
Major Arcana

The heart of the
matter

3)
Major Arcana

How it manifests

Practical action
to take

4)
Emotional –
Cups
Follow your
intuition

5)
Inspirational –
Wands
Find the good
in everything

6)
Intellectual-
Swords
Enlist help &
advice from
others

7)
Physical –
Pentacles
How it manifests
physically

Created by Winslow Eliot

23- Setting a Goal

The **Setting a Goal** spread is a no-nonsense, practical spread that will clearly show you how to position yourself for success in any endeavor.

Setting a Goal

Question   Name
                                            Date
                                            Time
Feelings or Interpretation   Deck

1) My goal	2) Personal qualities that help me reach my goal	3) Personal qualities that keep me from reaching my goal	4) Action to take to successfully reach my goal

Created by Sheilaa Hite

24- The Desire Spread

The Desire Spread will help you identify and access the internal and external power that is at your disposal whenever you want to manifest a desire. It's great for learning what motivates, blocks and/or guides you in making your dreams come true.

The Desire Spread

Question

Feelings or Interpretation

Name
Date
Time
Deck

1)
My
Desire

2)
What my
desire really
represents to
me

3)
Major Arcana

Self-confidence
(Warrior)

4)
Major Arcana

Self-doubt
(Dragon)

5)
What cards 3 & 4
reveal about me

6)
Major Arcana
(Guide)
The power that
this knowledge
gives me

7)
How to use this
power to
achieve my
desire
(with card 8)

8)
How to use this
power to achieve
my desire
(with card 7)

25- How Do I Manifest What I Want?

The **How Do I Manifest What I Want?** spread goes into detail about who you are, what you want and how to make it happen.

How Do I Manifest What I Want?

Question

Name
Date
Time

Feelings or Interpretation

Deck

1)
Querent
or
What you want
to manifest

2)
Directions from
the Universe

Cards 2 & 3

3)
Directions from
the Universe

Cards 2 & 3

4)
Action required
to manifest what
you want

Cards 4, 5 & 6

5)
Action required
to manifest what
you want

Cards 4, 5 & 6

6)
Action required
to manifest what
you want

Cards 4, 5 & 6

7)
Resources
supporting this
action

8)
Obstacles
blocking this
action

9)
What you need
to release

10)
What you need
to accept

26- Key to Success Spread

The **Key to Success Spread** helps you unlock the secrets that will reveal what it takes to create a successful outcome to any enterprise.

Key to Success Spread

Question

Feelings or Interpretation

Name
Date
Time
Deck

1)
What can I
count on

4)
Who/what is
misleading me

7)
Major Arcana

Help from the
Universe

2)
What will set
me back

5)
Unforeseen
obstacle

8)
Main thing to
keep in mind

3)
What will move
me forward

6)
Unexpected
support

Created by Sheilaa Hite

27- The Gods Must be Crazy

The **Gods Must be Crazy** spread was inspired by the classic 1980 film of the same name. It can help you understand why and how you were chosen for 'amazing opportunity' and guide you in making the most of it.

The Gods Must be Crazy

Question   Name

Date

Time

Feelings or Interpretation   Deck

3)
Major Arcana

Why was I
chosen?

2)
Major Arcana

What part do I
play in this
opportunity?

6)
Major Arcana

How does this
new opportunity
reflect my personal
growth?

4)
Major Arcana

Who are my
allies?

1)
Major Arcana

Why is the
opportunity being
presented to me
now?

7)
Major Arcana

How is my karma
connected to where
I am now?

5)
Major Arcana

How can I
effectively own
my part in this?

Created by Sheilaa Hite

28- Your Mission

The **Your Mission** spread was inspired by the opening scene in the television series, "Mission Impossible." It's a good spread for guidance when you have a new or difficult task ahead of you.

Your Mission

Question

Name
Date
Time
Deck

Feelings or Interpretation

1)
Minor Arcana

Action required
to complete the
task

Cards 1, 2 & 3

2)
Minor Arcana

Action required to
complete the
task

Cards 1. 2 & 3

3)
Minor Arcana

Action required
to complete the
task

Cards 1, 2 & 3

4)
Major Arcana

Your safe space

5)
Major Arcana

Your Guide

6)
Major Arcana

The Mission

29- The Star Spread

The Star Spread was inspired by renowned intuitive counselor, DearJames™. It brings all of the necessary elements together for achieving goals, completing projects and making a better life for yourself. It's especially good for answering the question, "What do I need to do in this situation in order to achieve my desired outcome?"

***It's a very good omen if The Star card appears in the spread.*

The Star Spread

Question

Feelings or Interpretation

Name
Date
Time
Deck

3)
GRATITUDE
What aspect of my life experiences can I give thanks to for preparing me for this moment?

2)
INTENTION
How committed am I to achieving my goal?

4)
FORGIVENESS
Who/what do I need to forgive in order to achieve my goal?

1)
PERMISSION
What do I need to be willing to be, do or have?

5)
SURRENDER
What do I need to let go of in order to achieve my goal?

Inspired by DearJames™
Created by Sheilaa Hite

30- The Treasure Hunt Spread

The **Treasure Hunt Spread** is a map that will assist you on your adventure as you seek and find the elements and aspects that will reveal the hiding place of whatever your heart wants to achieve.

The Treasure Hunt Spread

Question

Feelings or Interpretation

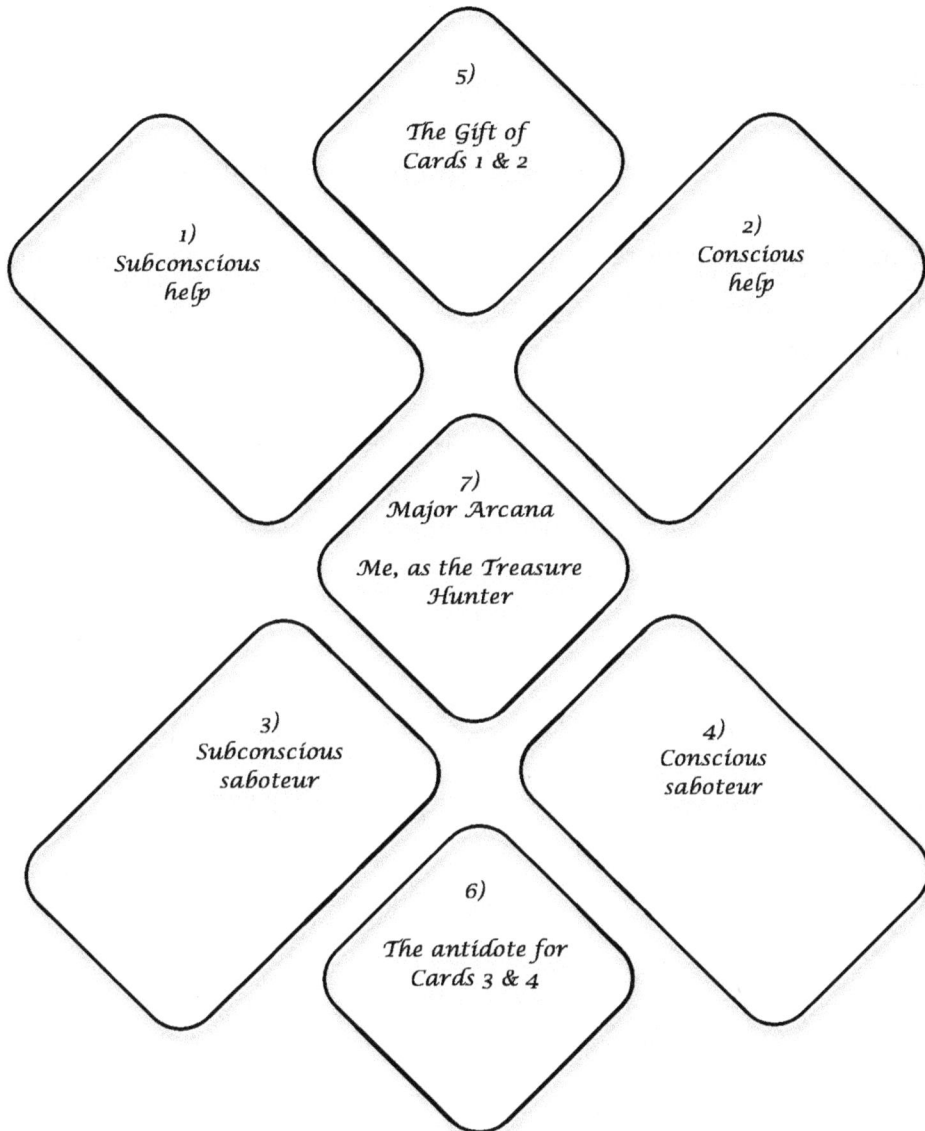

Name
Date
Time
Deck

5) The Gift of Cards 1 & 2

1) Subconscious help

2) Conscious help

7) Major Arcana

Me, as the Treasure Hunter

3) Subconscious saboteur

4) Conscious saboteur

6) The antidote for Cards 3 & 4

Created by Linda Farmer & Sheilaa Hite

31- Painting the Sistine Chapel

Painting the Sistine Chapel refers to your being inspired to create something lasting and meaningful; something impactful, regardless of what it is or of its size, that defines you and will remind you of your greatness.

Painting the Sistine Chapel
Lasting, Meaningful Creation

Question

Name
Date
Time
Deck

Feelings or Interpretation

7)
How to use
this power to
achieve your
desire

8)
The gift
that
achieving
your desire
gives you

6)
Major
Arcana

The power
that this
knowledge
gives you

5)
What #3
and #4
reveal about
you

3)
Self-doubt

4)
Self-
confidence

2)
What your
desire really
represents to
you

1)
Your desire

Created by Sheilaa Hite

Know Thyself

"In the infinity of creation, there are infinite possibilities. For as long as there have been beings capable of making choices, we have steered our own reality."

Anonymous

32- What is My Life's Purpose?

The **What is My Life's Purpose?** spread is awesome. How many times have you asked yourself that question? My students and I were amazed at how accurately we could see ourselves and our paths. This spread is connected to the **My Karma** spread.

What is My Life's Purpose?

Question

Name
Date
Time

Feelings or Interpretation

Deck

1)
Major Arcana

What is my life's
purpose?

2)
Minor Arcana

Am I fulfilling my
life's purpose?

3)
Minor Arcana

What do I need to do
to fulfill my life's
purpose?

6)
Minor Arcana

How do I access and
share my gifts and
talents with the
world?

4)
Major Arcana

What are my hidden
gifts/talents?

5)
Major Arcana

What are my
obvious
gifts/talents?

7)
Major Arcana

How is my karma
connected to my
life's purpose?

33- The Defining Moment

The Defining Moment spread is revealing, dynamic and transformational. A defining moment is a pivotal point in your development/life. It's the moment that makes you special as a result of having made an important choice or decision.

The Defining Moment

Question How can I consciously recognize, own
and activate this defining moment?

Name

Date

Time

Deck

Feelings or Interpretation

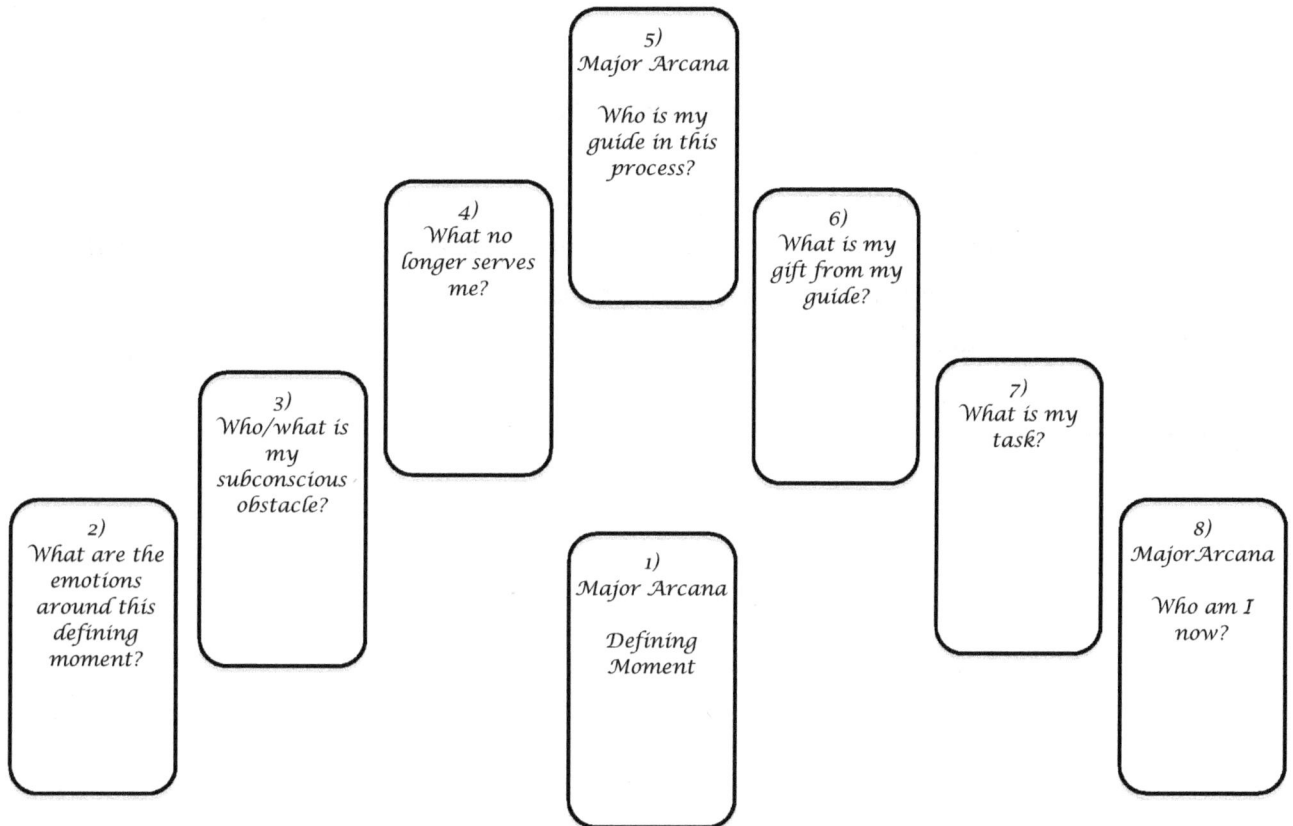

5)
Major Arcana

Who is my
guide in this
process?

4)
What no
longer serves
me?

6)
What is my
gift from my
guide?

3)
Who/what is
my
subconscious
obstacle?

7)
What is my
task?

2)
What are the
emotions
around this
defining
moment?

1)
Major Arcana

Defining
Moment

8)
Major Arcana

Who am I
now?

Created by Sheilaa Hite

34- Personal Power Spread

The **Personal Power Spread** is both specific and versatile. Ask the question, "What is my Personal Power this lifetime?" and you'll get an understanding of how you best operate in life. Ask, "What is my Personal Power in this situation?" and you'll get an excellent picture of your power in that situation.

Personal Power Spread

Question

Feelings or Interpretation

Name
Date
Time
Deck

```
              ┌──────────────┐
              │      3)      │
              │ Logical mind,│
              │Consciousness │
              │              │
              └──────────────┘

┌──────────────┐                        ┌──────────────┐
│     2)       │                        │      4)      │
│  Intuition,  │                        │  Physical    │
│ Subconscious │                        │  expression, │
│              │                        │outcome, lesson│
│              │      ┌──────────────┐  │              │
└──────────────┘      │      6)      │  └──────────────┘
                      │ Heart of the │
                      │   Matter     │
                      │              │
┌──────────────┐      │              │  ┌──────────────┐
│     1)       │      └──────────────┘  │      5)      │
│Message from the│                       │  Spiritual   │
│   Universe   │                        │  expression, │
│              │                        │outcome, lesson│
│              │                        │              │
└──────────────┘                        └──────────────┘
```

Created by Sheilaa Hite

35- I Am

The **I Am** spread is such an important spread because it clearly shows you who you are and how the Divine Power sees you as opposed to what you've come to believe about yourself. Use it in different situations to understand how to best use your power.

I Am

Question

Name
Date
Time

Feelings or Interpretation

Deck

Major Arcana

Who I _think_ I am

Major Arcana

Who I _really_ am

36- As Others See Me

The **As Others See Me** spread was inspired by the great Scottish poet, Robert Burns. This spread gives us the gift of peering into the looking glass and, at last, clearly seeing ourselves and the impact we have on our world.

As Others See Me

"Oh wad some Power the gift tae gie us, to see oursels as ithers see us."

Robert Burns

Question

Name

Date

Time

Feelings or Interpretation

Deck

4)
What will result
from the
combination

3)
How to combine
the 2 perceptions

5)
Light side of the
combination

2)
(Major Arcana)
How others
see me

6)
Shadow side of the
combination

1)
(Major Arcana)
How I see myself

7)
The gift of the
combination

37- Que Sera, Sera Spread

The **Que Sera, Sera Spread** was inspired by the old classic song that asked, "When I grow up, what will I become?" We all had a vision when we were five years old that helped shape us into who we are today—what was yours?

Que Sera, Sera Spread

Question

Name
Date
Time
Deck

Feelings or Interpretation

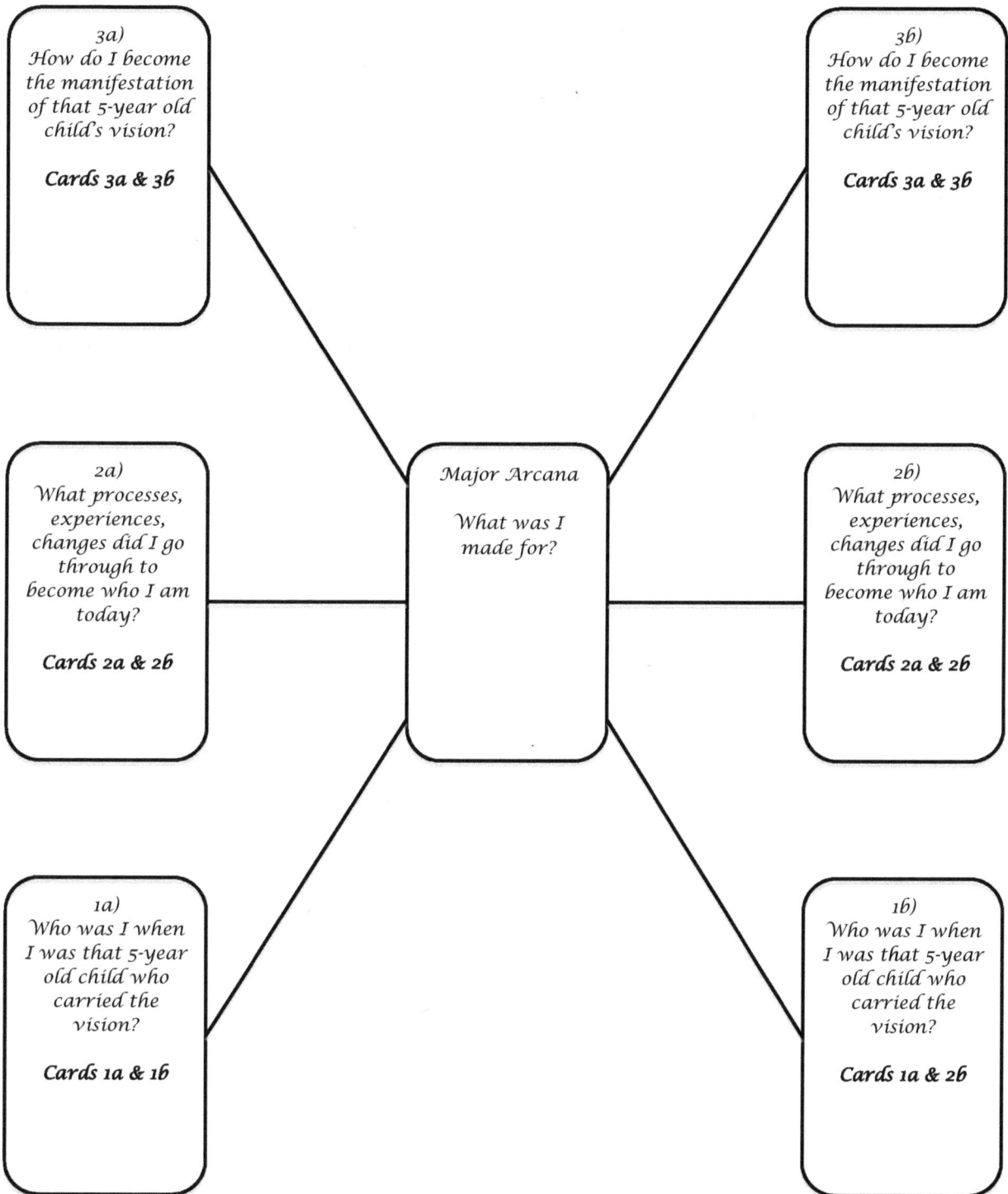

3a)
How do I become the manifestation of that 5-year old child's vision?

Cards 3a & 3b

3b)
How do I become the manifestation of that 5-year old child's vision?

Cards 3a & 3b

2a)
What processes, experiences, changes did I go through to become who I am today?

Cards 2a & 2b

Major Arcana

What was I made for?

2b)
What processes, experiences, changes did I go through to become who I am today?

Cards 2a & 2b

1a)
Who was I when I was that 5-year old child who carried the vision?

Cards 1a & 1b

1b)
Who was I when I was that 5-year old child who carried the vision?

Cards 1a & 2b

Created by Sheilaa Hite

38- Serenity Spread

The **Serenity Spread** was inspired by the iconic prayer attributed to a minister in the 1940's. It really helps us to see and properly use our power in all kinds of situations so that the best outcome can be achieved.

Serenity Spread

Question

Feelings or Interpretation

Name
Date
Time
Deck

3)
What I can
change, do, control

2)
What I can't
change, do, control

4)
Alternative actions
available to me

6)
Heart of the Matter

The gift in this
situation

1)
Problem

5)
Spiritual
expression,
outcome, lesson

Created by Sheilaa Hite

39- What Was I Made For?

The **What Was I Made For?** spread offers us another way of looking at ourselves and our life's purpose by revealing our natural gifts and talents to us.

What Was I Made For?

Question

Feelings or Interpretation

Name
Date
Time
Deck

3)
What passion guides me at this time?

2)
What do I need to allow?

4)
My natural gifts & talents

6)
Heart of the Matter

1)
Major Arcana

Message from the Universe

5)
What is the most beneficial way to use my natural gifts & talents

40- Guiding Energy Spread

The **Guiding Energy Spread.** What expression of energy guides you through the experiences that characterize you and your life? In addition to the basic energy, there is also a different expression of energy that directs and guides you through each experience. This spread can be used to determine the most powerful energies in your life at any given time.

Guiding Energy Spread

Question

Feelings or Interpretation

Name
Date
Time
Deck

3)
Major Arcana

What energetic
force guides me?

1)
What
subconscious
energy is
present?

5)

Heart of the
Matter

2)
What conscious
energy is
present?

4)
What energetic
force led me to
where I am now?

Created by Linda Farmer
Inspired by Sheilaa Hite

41- Flying My Freak Flag

The **Flying My Freak Flag** spread was inspired by musician, philosopher and deeply magical being, Jimi Hendrix. Your freak flag is that aspect of you that makes you different, that separates you from the mundane complacency of life.

Flying My Freak Flag
An Homage to St. Jimi

Question

Name
Date
Time

Feelings or Interpretation

Deck

1)
Flag Pole & Flag

What stabilizes my self-expression

2)
Flag

What makes me an original

3)
Flag

What encourages me to be true to myself

4)
Flag Pole

What supports me and my uniqueness
Cards 4, 5 & 6

5)
Flag Pole

What supports me and my uniqueness
Cards 4, 5 & 6

6)
Flag Pole

What supports me and my uniqueness
Cards 4, 5 & 6

Inspired by Jimi Hendrix
Created by Sheilaa Hite

42- My Values Spread

The **My Values Spread** will show you how relevant the values you learned from your family of origin and from your own life experience are to you in your current life.

My Values Spread

Feelings or Interpretation

3)
How both sets of
values conflict
with each other

2)
How my chosen
values affected
me

4)
How both sets of
values confirm
each other

1)
How my family's
values affected
me

8)
Major Arcana

My Life Path
Card

5)
How relevant are
my family's values
to my current life?

7)
How does my
current life
reflect my true
values?

6)
What family
values no longer
serve me

Created by Sheilaa Hite

43- Sunlight and Shadow Spread

The **Sunlight and Shadow Spread** lets you see the difference between your light side (your conscious side) and your shadow side (your unconscious side) at play in your life in their various forms.

Sunlight and Shadow Spread

Question   Name
                                                            Date
                                                            Time
Feelings or Interpretation   Deck

1) (Physical) My light side	2) (Physical) My shadow side	3) (Mental) My light side	4) (Mental) My shadow side
5) (Emotional) My light side	6) (Emotional) My shadow side	7) (Spiritual) My light side	8) (Spiritual) My shadow side

9)
What aids me in
developing my
light side

10)
What hinders me
in developing my
light side

11)
Outcome of
developing my
light side

Created by Sheilaa Hite

44- Defining Myself

The **Defining Myself** spread is powerful and enlightening. It shows you who and where you are now and helps you to pinpoint your essence in a one word description.

Defining Myself

Question   Name
                                            Date
                                            Time
Feelings or Interpretation   Deck

1)
I AM

3)
What I
understand
about myself

5)
My greatest
personal asset

7)
Most stable
aspect of myself

9)
I AM, in a
word...

8)
Least stable aspect
of myself

6)
My greatest
personal liability

4)
What I don't
understand
about myself

2)
I am not

Created by Sheilaa Hite

45- Inner Strength Spread

The **Inner Strength Spread** shows you the source of your inner strength and self-confidence as well as what can cause those two great aspects of yourself to fail to support you.

Inner Strength Spread

Question   Name
                                                            Date
                                                            Time
Feelings or Interpretation   Deck

2)
Source of my
courage

1)
Source of my
Inner Strength

3)
Source of my
fearfulness

4)
Source of my
self-confidence

5)
What undermines
my self-confidence

6)
Action that
restores my self-
confidence

8)
Aspect of
myself I can
always count
on

7)
My sense of
personal
responsibility

46- The Core Issues Spread

The Core Issues Spread is another spread that helps you identify, access and use your innate and most powerful qualities in order to fulfill your destiny.

The Core Issues Spread

Question

Feelings or Interpretation

Name
Date
Time
Deck

1)
Major Arcana

My core issues

2)
My greatest
weakness

3)
Major Arcana

How I can
access my
Power

4)
My greatest fear

5)
Major Arcana

How I can access
my Courage

6)
My greatest
strength

7)
Major Arcana

How I can access
& utilize my full
Strength

47- Sum Total of All Our Parts

The **Sum Total of All Our Parts** spread is a great assessment of who you are, where you came from and what skills you possess at this time in your life.

Sum Total of All Our Parts

Question

Feelings or Interpretation

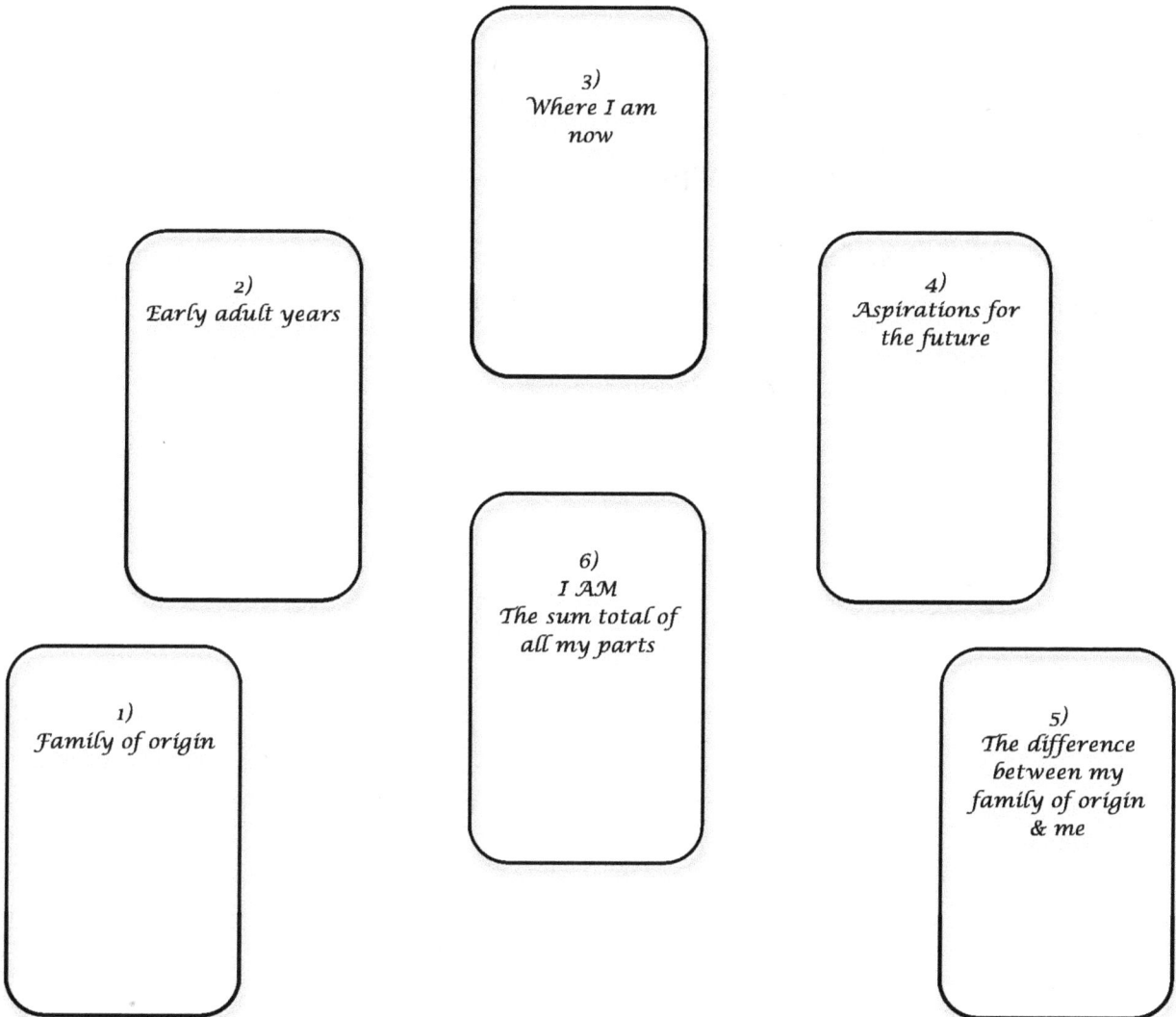

Name
Date
Time
Deck

```
        ┌─────────────┐
        │     3)      │
        │ Where I am  │
        │    now      │
        └─────────────┘

┌─────────────┐              ┌─────────────┐
│     2)      │              │     4)      │
│ Early adult │              │ Aspirations │
│   years     │              │ for the     │
│             │              │  future     │
└─────────────┘              └─────────────┘

        ┌─────────────┐
        │     6)      │
        │   I AM      │
        │ The sum     │
        │ total of    │
        │ all my parts│
        └─────────────┘

┌─────────────┐              ┌─────────────┐
│     1)      │              │     5)      │
│  Family of  │              │ The         │
│   origin    │              │ difference  │
│             │              │ between my  │
│             │              │ family of   │
│             │              │ origin & me │
└─────────────┘              └─────────────┘
```

Created by Sheilaa Hite

48- Aspects of Myself Spread

The **Aspects of Myself Spread** will help you clearly and consciously inventory the different aspects of your personality that have power in your life at any given time.

Aspects of Myself Spread

Question

Name
Date
Time
Deck

Feelings or Interpretation

1) Naive	1a) Cynical
2) Feminine	2a) Masculine
	6) Major Arcana Combined, I am...	
3) Responsible	3a) Irresponsible
	7) Minor Arcana How I express the best in myself	
4) Warrior	4a) Peace Keeper
5) Emotional	5a) Logical

Created by Sheilaa Hite

49- Authenticity Spread

The **Authenticity Spread**. Being who you were meant to be and being true to that self is what will help you to live an authentic and satisfying life.

Authenticity Spread

Name
Date
Time
Deck

Feelings or Interpretation

1)
How I connect
with my
authenticity

4)
How I express
my authenticity

2)
What happens
when I'm most
inauthentic

7)
My Authenticity

My Major Arcana
Life Path Card

5)
What being
inauthentic creates
for me

3)
What happens
when I'm most
authentic

6)
What being
authentic creates
for me

Created by Sheilaa Hite

50- My Life Experience Toolkit Spread

The **My Life Experience Toolkit Spread** is another wonderfully enlightening spread that will show you what your strengths and weaknesses are and how to empower and use them to enhance the quality of your life. It can be used to learn who you basically are and it can be used whenever you want to know what resources you bring to any situation.

My Life Experience Toolkit Spread

Question

Name
Date
Time
Deck

Feelings or Interpretation

1)
My strengths &
skills

1a)
My weaknesses &
vices

2)
Old restricting
issues

2a)
New liberating
beginnings

6)
Major Arcana

My starting
point

3)
Unknown talents

3a)
Natural abilities

7)
Proof that my
passions are
worthwhile

4)
Doubts & fears

4a)
Faith &
courage

5)
Intuitive &
insightful

5a)
Logical &
analytical

51- To Thine Own Self Be True Spread

The **To Thine Own Self Be True Spread** shows you what you need to know yourself and do in order to follow Shakespeare's wisest admonition.

To Thine Own Self Be True Spread

Question

Feelings or Interpretation

Name
Date
Time
Deck

1)
How I think I
feel about myself

7)
What I need to
focus on now

2)
How I really feel
about myself

8)
Major Arcana
The message from
the Universe

6)
What I need to
accept
about myself

3)
How I'm true to
myself

5)
What I need to
acknowledge
about myself

4)
How I'm not true
to myself

Cycles and Assessments

"I'll go anywhere as long as it's forward."
David Livingstone

52- After the Storm Spread

The **After the Storm Spread** was designed by one of my students who had survived the horrific Hurricane Sandy storm of 2012. She saw the event as a weather phenomenon and as a metaphor for the 'storms' we all go through in life.

After the Storm Spread

Question

Feelings or Interpretation

Name
Date
Time
Deck

1)
Major Arcana

How has this
challenging event
changed my life?

2)
What was
washed away in
the storm?

3)
What remains?

4)
What part of
myself was in the
dark?

6)
How has my
perspective been
changed by this
experience?

5)
How was I
enlightened by this
experience?

7)
Major Arcana

The most
beneficial way
to thrive in
this
environment
with this new
perspective

53- Mapping My Progress

The **Mapping My Progress** spread is a great little spread that quickly and powerfully helps to guide you to where you want to be at the end of a cycle, event or life passage.

Mapping My Progress

Question

Name
Date
Time

Feelings or Interpretation

Deck

1)
Where do I want
to be at the end
of this cycle or
experience?

2)
Who do I need to
be in order to get
there?

3)
How do I get
there?

Message from the
Universe

4)
How do I get
there?

Heart of the
Matter

5)
How do I get
there?

Spiritual &/or
Physical
expression or
lesson

Created by Sheilaa Hite

54- Birthday/New Year Spread

The **Birthday/New Year Spread** will give you a detailed overview of your year in the 12 months following your birthday or the beginning of any calendar New Year.

Birthday/New Year Spread

Question

Feelings or Interpretation

Name
Date
Time
Deck

1)
Major Arcana
Month 1
(January 1 or
birth month)
Querent poised to
enter new phase

12)
Major Arcana
What this year is
about for querent
and
Month 12

2)
Month 2

6)
Month 6
Influenced by
months
2 & 3

9)
Month 9
Influenced by
months
2 & 3

3)
Month 3

7)
Month 7
Influenced by
months
3 & 4

10)
Month 10
Influenced by
months
3 & 4

4)
Month 4

8)
Month 8
Influenced by
months
4 & 5

11)
Month 11
Influenced by
months
4 & 5

5)
Month 5

Created by Sheilaa Hite

55- End of Year or Cycle Assessment Spread

The **End of Year or Cycle Assessment Spread** gives you a review of what you've experienced and how you've grown during a recently passed year, cycle or event.

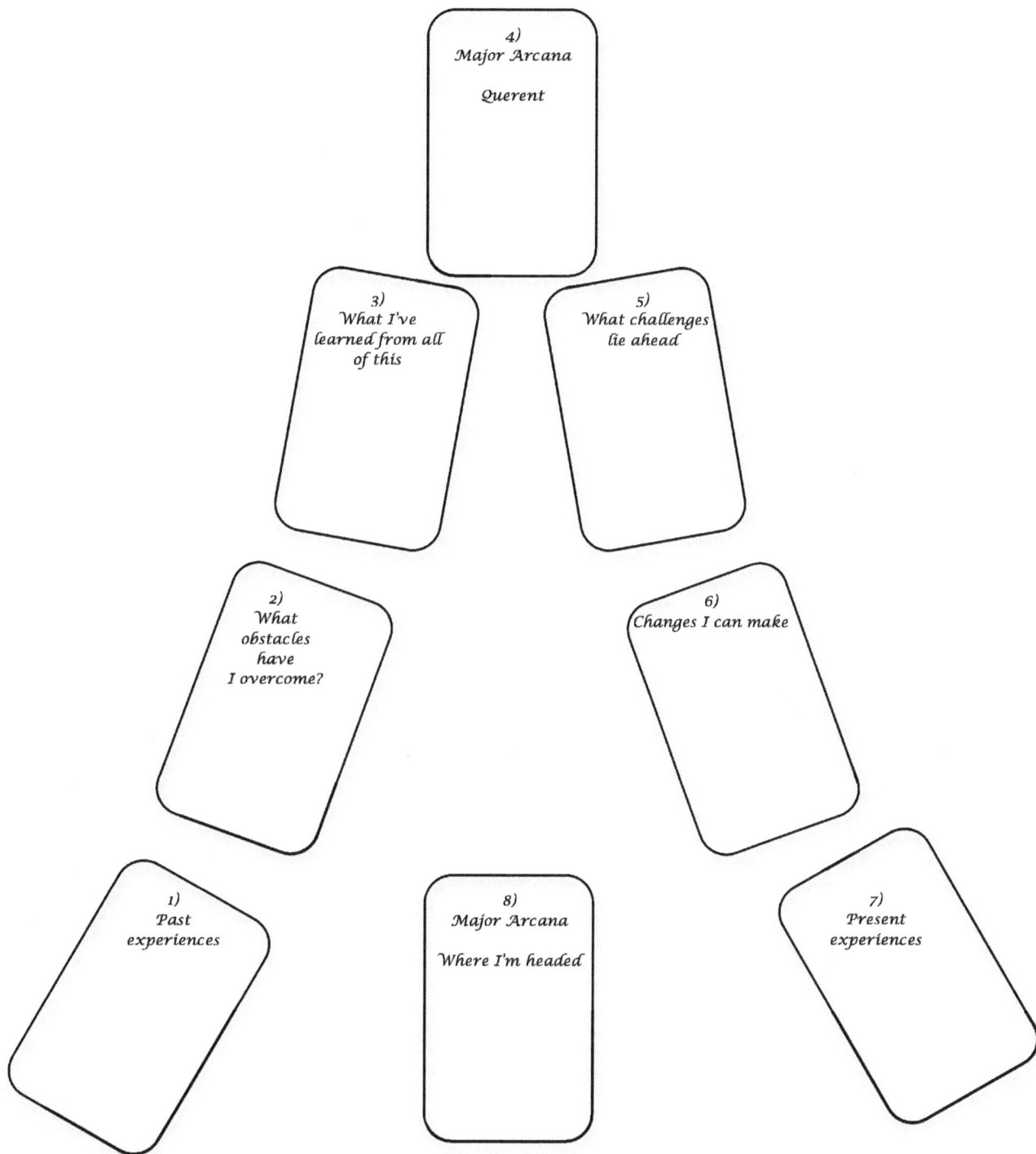

End of Year or Cycle Assessment Spread

Question   Name
                                                            Date
                                                            Time
Feelings or Interpretation   Deck

4)
Major Arcana

Querent

3)
What I've
learned from all
of this

5)
What challenges
lie ahead

2)
What
obstacles
have
I overcome?

6)
Changes I can make

1)
Past
experiences

8)
Major Arcana

Where I'm headed

7)
Present
experiences

Created by Sheilaa Hite

56- New Year Spread

The **New Year Spread** is another great assessment tool. Use it at the start of any of the calendar and personal New Year beginnings that we all relate to (January 1st, Chinese New Year, Spring, May Day, any religious New Year, your birthday).

New Year Spread

Question

Feelings or Interpretation

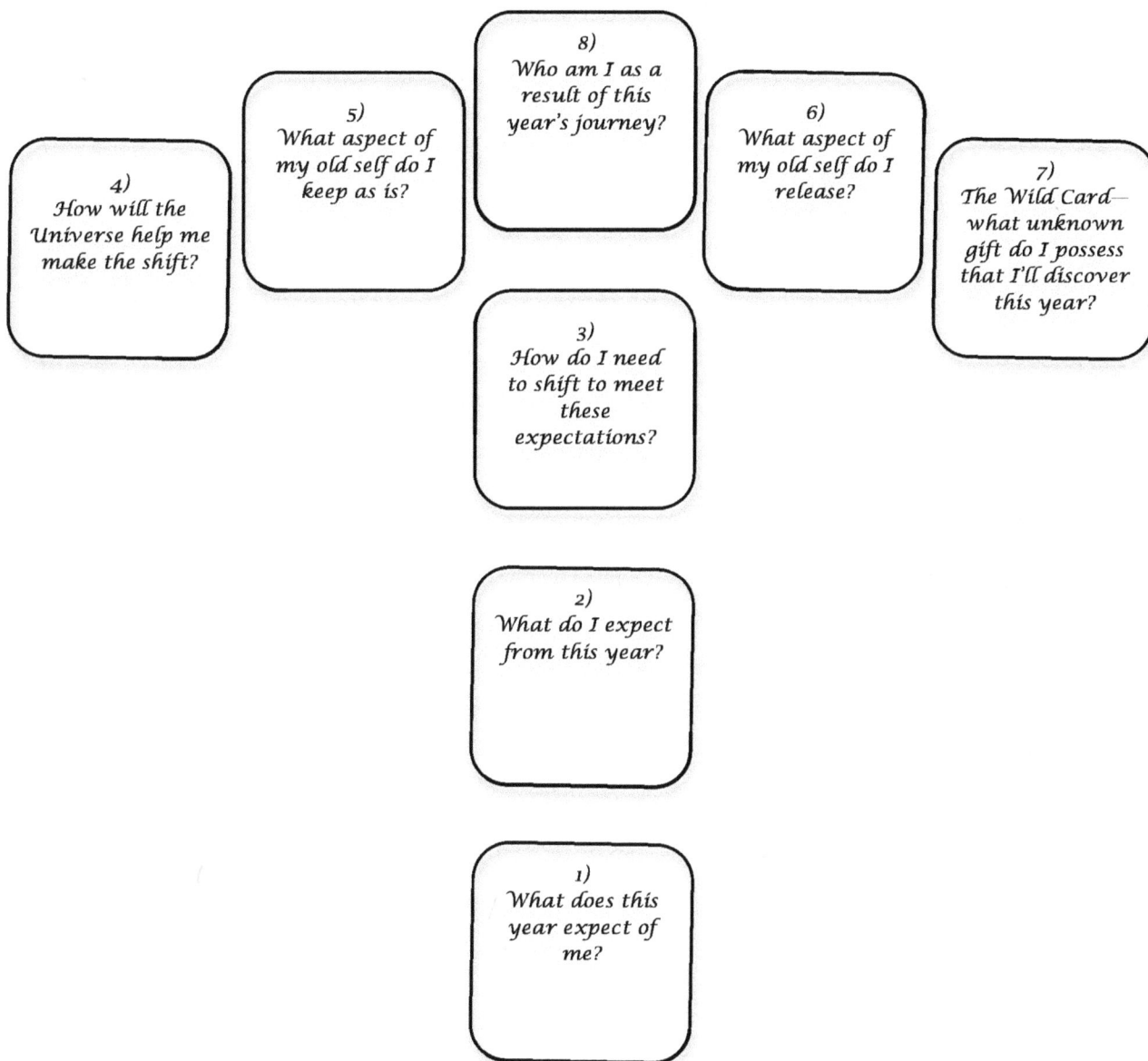

Name
Date
Time
Deck

8)
Who am I as a result of this year's journey?

5)
What aspect of my old self do I keep as is?

6)
What aspect of my old self do I release?

4)
How will the Universe help me make the shift?

7)
The Wild Card— what unknown gift do I possess that I'll discover this year?

3)
How do I need to shift to meet these expectations?

2)
What do I expect from this year?

1)
What does this year expect of me?

Created by Sheilaa Hite

Past Lives and Karma

"A little while, a moment of rest upon the wind,
and another woman shall bear me."
Kahlil Gibran

57- "Have We Met?"

The **"Have We Met?"** spread is the quintessential past-life recognition spread. We've all met someone whom we feel an instant kinship with or antipathy toward. With this spread you can finally figure out if you want to continue the relationship or head for the hills!

"Have We Met?"
Past Life Relationships

Question

Name
Date
Time
Deck

Feelings or Interpretation

2)
How we perceive
each other

3)
What are we to
avoid or move
beyond?

1)
What is our
connection?

(If a Major
Arcana card, it's
karmic)

4)
What are we to
accomplish?

5)
Where do we go
from here?

Created by Sheilaa Hite

58- My Karma

The **My Karma** spread is patterned after a set of scales with Major Arcana cards acting as the fulcrum that balances Fate and Destiny. It's a perfect mirror for seeing the results of the choices you make and the roads you're taking in life. Linked with the spread, **What is My Life's Purpose?**, it's remarkable in the way it reveals our personal truth to us.

My Karma

Question   Name
                                                            Date
                                                            Time
Feelings or Interpretation   Deck

1)
Major Arcana

*My Karma,
Destiny or Fate.
What I'm here to
balance*

2)
Major Arcana

*Divine Overview/
Guidance
How do I balance
my karma?*

5)
*How settling for
fate blocks,
enslaves, weakens
me*

6)
*How creating my
own destiny
liberates, brings
opportunities,
empowers me*

3)
Major Arcana

*How is my karma
connected to my
life's purpose?*

7)
*Hidden,
unconscious
manifestations*

8)
*Obvious
manifestations*

9)
*Hidden,
subconscious
manifestations*

10)
*Conscious
manifestations*

4)
*Foundation;
main form or
type of
karmic issues*

FATE
*What you have to accept in life if you
don't balance your karma. How you
surrender your power. Your weaknesses.*

DESTINY
*What you can make of your life if you
balance your karma. How you own &
benefit from your power. Your strengths.*

Created by Sheilaa Hite

59- Karma Crossroad

The **Karma Crossroad** spread gives us what we all want in life—a choice. It's so exciting to see that I can take a different path and what's likely to happen if I do. For such a 'heavy' topic, working with this spread created so much joy for my students and me. In addition to answering the question at the top of the form, you can also ask about your karma with any person or situation.

Karma Crossroad

Question

Feelings or Interpretation

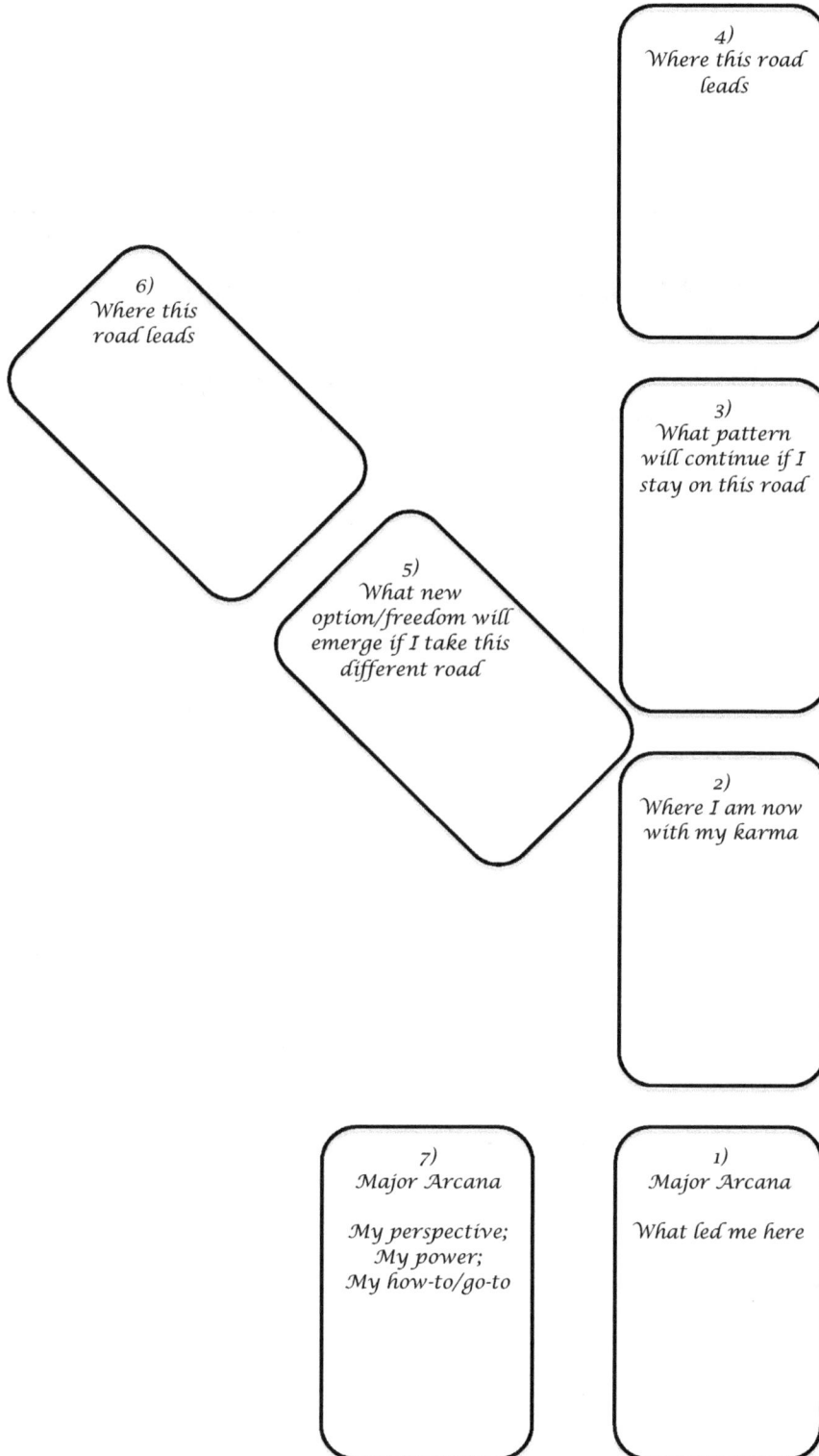

Name
Date
Time
Deck

4)
Where this road
leads

6)
Where this
road leads

3)
What pattern
will continue if I
stay on this road

5)
What new
option/freedom will
emerge if I take this
different road

2)
Where I am now
with my karma

7)
Major Arcana

My perspective;
My power;
My how-to/go-to

1)
Major Arcana

What led me here

Created by Linda Farmer and Sheilaa Hite

60- Why Does This Keep Happening?

The **Why Does This Keep Happening?** spread answers the age-old question that always seems to accompany some powerful messaging experiences from the Universe.

Why Does This Keep Happening?

Question

Name
Date
Time
Deck

Feelings or Interpretation

1) Is this a past life issue? (If a Major Arcana card appears here, it's a past life issue)	2) True nature of this issue	3) My part in this issue	4) Most important thing to keep in mind regarding this issue

61- How Can I Change Negative Karma?

The **How Can I Change Negative Karma?** spread. This is a question I get asked a lot, especially when people are undergoing a lot of stress in their lives. This spread delivers the answer in a simple straightforward manner.

How Can I Change Negative Karma?

Question

Name
Date
Time

Feelings or Interpretation

Deck

1)
How this negative karmic pattern disrupts my life

2)
The lessons I've learned through dealing with this pattern

3)
The action required to change this negative pattern

62- All the Lifetimes... Reincarnation Spread

The **All the Lifetimes... Reincarnation Spread** reveals a person's quality puts into perspective what we've become and how our accumulated lifetimes have and continue to shape us. It reveals a person's quality

All the Lifetimes... Reincarnation Spread

Question

Name
Date
Time
Deck

Feelings or Interpretation

3)
What I got right

5)
How I must
atone

1)
What/how I was

7)
My current life

8)
How my past life
affects my
current life

2)
What/how I am
today

4)
What I got
wrong

6)
What I must
learn

63- How Do My Past Lives Influence My Current Life?

The **How Do My Past Lives Influence My Current Life?** spread is short, simple and deep. The soulful quality of the answers that come out of laying this spread never ceases to amaze me.

How Do My Past Lives Influence My Current Life?

Question

Feelings or Interpretation

Name

Date

Time

Deck

```
1)
My past
influences
```

```
2)
My current life
expressions based
on past life
influences
```

```
3)
My future—
where I'm headed
```

Choices and Options

"We are our choices."
Jean-Paul Sartre

64- Clarifying Options Spread

The **Clarifying Options Spread** will make it easy for you to sort through the most significant points of any issue where options are a factor in the decision making process.

Clarifying Options Spread

Question

Feelings or Interpretation

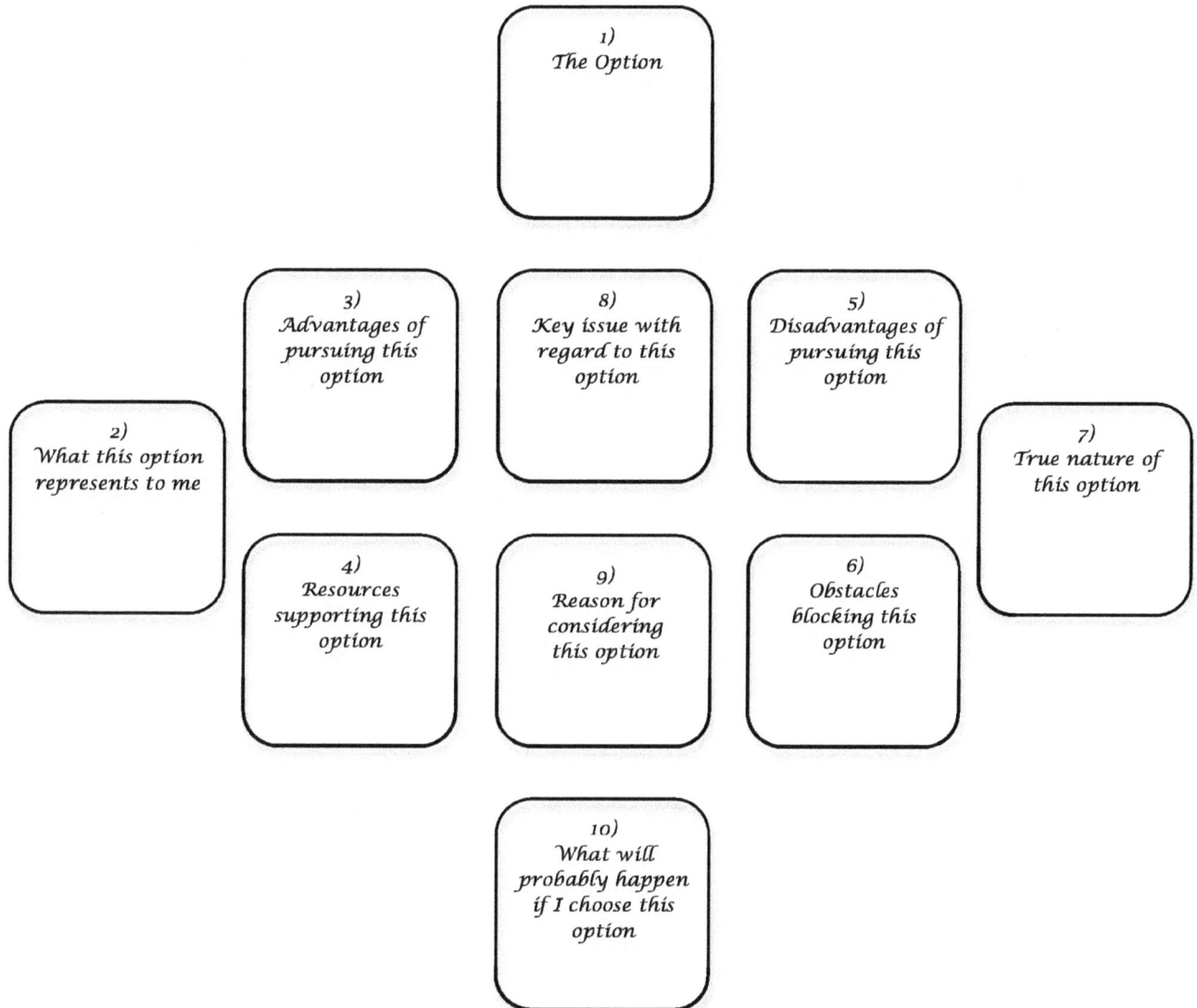

Name
Date
Time
Deck

1)
The Option

3)
Advantages of
pursuing this
option

8)
Key issue with
regard to this
option

5)
Disadvantages of
pursuing this
option

2)
What this option
represents to me

7)
True nature of
this option

4)
Resources
supporting this
option

9)
Reason for
considering
this option

6)
Obstacles
blocking this
option

10)
What will
probably happen
if I choose this
option

Created by Sheilaa Hite

65- Making Choices Spread

The **Making Choices Spread** is another good spread if you're wanting to figure out which is the more advantageous direction for you.

Making Choices Spread

Question

Name
Date
Time
Deck

Feelings or Interpretation

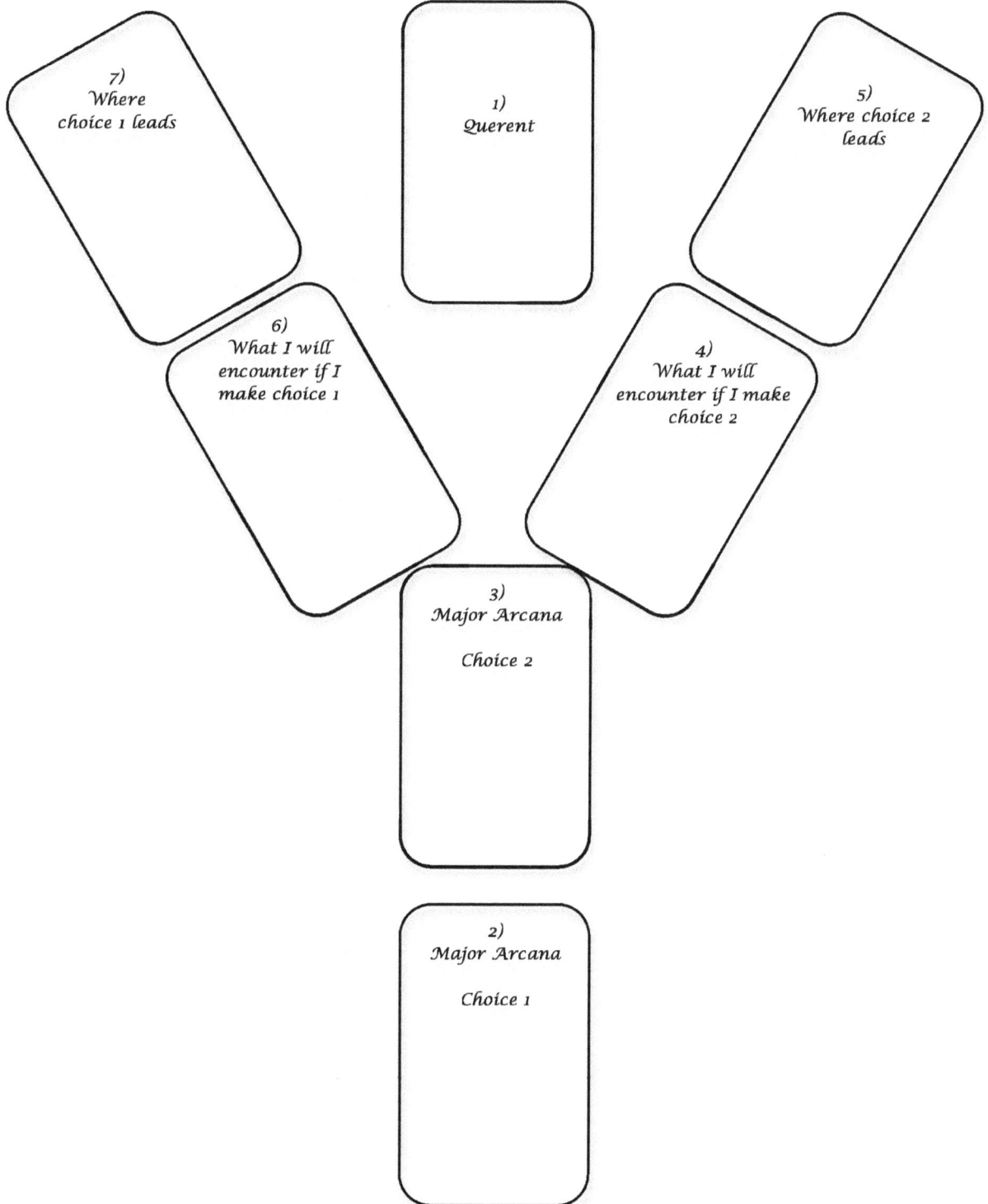

7)
Where
choice 1 leads

1)
Querent

5)
Where choice 2
leads

6)
What I will
encounter if I
make choice 1

4)
What I will
encounter if I make
choice 2

3)
Major Arcana

Choice 2

2)
Major Arcana

Choice 1

66- Examining My Options Spread

The **Examining My Options Spread** provides a very straight forward examination of any two options while giving you instructions on the most beneficial action for you to take regarding them.

Examining My Options Spread

Question

Name
Date
Time
Deck

Feelings or Interpretation

1)
Option 1
Positive Aspects

2)
Option 1
Negative Aspects

5)
Option 2
Positive Aspects

6)
Option 2
Negative Aspects

3)
True nature of
this option

7)
True nature of
this option

4)
Action I need to
take regarding
this option

8)
Action I need to
take regarding
this option

Personal Growth

"The ultimate measure of a man is not where he stands in moments of comfort,
but where he stands at times of challenge and controversy."
Dr. Martin Luther King, Jr

67- 5 Stages of Grief

The **5 Stages of Grief** spread is based on the work of Dr. Elisabeth Kubler-Ross. To help you understand and move through the loss of a person, relationship, job, era, loved one or any of the other myriad transitions we experience in our lives, meditate and journal on each card you pull for this spread.

5 Stages of Grief

Question

Feelings or Interpretation

Name
Date
Time
Deck

3)

Denial

2)

Shock

4)

Bargaining

1)

Anger

6)

Major Arcana

Who you've
become as a
result of this
experience

5)

Acceptance

Created by Jennifer Lamb

68- The Fear Not Spread

The Fear Not Spread will help you dispel the debilitating effects of the energy of fear as it shows you how to move into the powerful space of your heart and courage.

The Fear Not Spread

Question

Name
Date
Time
Deck

Feelings or Interpretation

1)
What you fear
about expressing
your heart to the
world

2)
Why you are
afraid of being
yourself

3)
Your true
connection to
your heart and
source of your
courage

4)
Action required to
live courageously

5)
Major Arcana

Your 'courage'
mentor

69- Dragon Slayer Spread

The **Dragon Slayer Spread** is one of your most important allies whenever you want to achieve a goal. It helps you consciously identify and enlist all of the elements necessary for your success.

Dragon Slayer Spread

Question

Name
Date
Time
Deck

Feelings or Interpretation

6)
Victory

Your reward

4)
Sacrifice

What you must
release

5)
Gifts

What you discover
or receive

1)
Your Quest

2)
Dragons

Obstacles

3)
Your allies

70- What We Resist, Persists

The **What We Resist, Persists** spread is one of my favorites! It so clearly holds up a mirror to our own participation in the deterioration or the advancement of our lives.

What We Resist, Persists

Question

Name
Date
Time
Deck

Feelings or Interpretation

1)
Major Arcana

What part of me
is resistant?

2)
Conscious reason
for resistance

4)
How I benefit
from resistance

3)
Unconscious
reason for
resistance

5)
What would
happen if the
resistance stays
in place

7)
What is behind
the resistance?
(Often a past-life
related reason)

6)
What would
happen if I
move through
resistance

8)
Major Arcana

Who will help
guide me through
this resistance?

9)
How will my
life be different
if I move
through the
resistance?

Created by Louise Rossi-Edwards

71- My Journey Continues… Spread

The **My Journey Continues… Spread** is a great for showing you how far you've come on your quest for a satisfying life. If the 9 of Cups appears in the spread, it's an indication that you're receiving powerful help from your Guides.

My Journey Continues... Spread

Question

Feelings or Interpretation

Name
Date
Time
Deck

1)
A wish that has
been fulfilled

2)
A longing that is
still with me

3)
A fear that is
dissipating

4)
The force that
carries me

5)
The new
beginning that
awaits me

Created by Sheilaa Hite

72- The Evolvement Spread

The Evolvement Spread is great for tracing the origins of your belief and behavioral systems and the effects they have on you.

The Evolvement Spread

Question

Feelings or Interpretation

Name
Date
Time
Deck

1)
Major Arcana

Who am I today?

1a)
Minor Arcana

Who am I today?

5)
Who is my
mother to me?

8)
Who is my
father to me?

2)
Major Arcana

The transforming
catalyst that
helped me evolve

6)
Positive impact
of my mother
on me

9)
Positive impact
of my father
on me

3)
How the
impact of both
my parents
essentially
affect me

7)
Negative impact
of my mother
on me

10)
Negative
impact of my
father
on me

4)
Major Arcana

What was my
essential nature
at birth?

Created by Louise Rossi-Edwards

73- Moving On Spread

The **Moving On Spread** lays everything about a particular situation out on the table and helps you to know how and what the situation taught you.

Moving On Spread

Question

Name
Date
Time
Deck

Feelings or Interpretation

1)
This part of my
experience is
over & done with

2)
This part of my
experience is
over but the
effects linger on

3)
What I expect
from my future

4)
What I don't expect
from my future

5)
What my future
holds

6)
What I've
learned from this
experience

Created by Sheilaa Hite

74- A Profound Experience-- Transformation

The **A Profound Experience-- Transformation** spread helps you to be more fully aware of just how much the experience impacted you and the direction of your life.

A Profound Experience-- Transformation

Question

Feelings or Interpretation

Name
Date
Time
Deck

5)
How will this transformation manifest in my life?

2)
How/who was I before the transformational experience?

1)
Heart of the matter

3)
How/who am I now because of the transformational experience?

4)
What is my responsibility to this transformation?

75- Hero's Journey Spread

The **Hero's Journey Spread** is inspired by Joseph Campbell's work. Whenever we set off on a quest, we need to be mindful that the objective of the adventure is always more than the prize that inspired us.

Hero's Journey Spread

Question

Feelings or Interpretation

Name
Date
Time
Deck

1)
The quest

What attracts
your interest

6)
Illusion

What distracts
you

7)
Major Arcana

The Holy Grail—
the Prize

2)
Major Arcana

Dragons--- Self-
wound or shadow

8)
Major Arcana

Your core task

5)
Major Arcana

Outside
challenges

9)
Major Arcana

The hero you've
become at quest's
end

3)
Allies--
What/who assists
you

4)
How you must
assist yourself

Created by Sheilaa Hite

76- The Alignment Spread

The Alignment Spread. We all need to be reminded to stay in proper, supportive alignment to our current environment and our goals. This spread will act as an important signpost on your journey and help you stay in alignment with your higher purpose and the intention the Universe has for you.

The Alignment Spread

Question   Name
                                                      Date
                                                      Time
Feelings or Interpretation   Deck

8)
Major Arcana

My ideal
alignment
reflecting the
Universal Source

5)
Stabilizing
alignment energy

6)
Main thing to
keep in mind
regarding
staying centered
and aligned

7)
Next overall
state of
alignment on all
levels

1)
My current
alignment

Mentally

2)
My current
alignment

Emotionally

3)
My current
alignment

Physically

4)
My current
alignment

Spiritually

Created by Sheilaa Hite

77- Personal Path Spread

The **Personal Path Spread** is great for marking your progress on your life-map. Your Major Arcana Life Path represents the essence of who you are and is your own unique vehicle transporting you along your path.

Personal Path Spread

Question

Name
Date
Time
Deck

Feelings or Interpretation

1)
What do I think I
need to leave
behind?

2)
What do I really
need to leave
behind?

3)
What am I
currently
embracing?

7)
My Major Arcana
Life Path Card

4)
What do I really
need to embrace?

5)
What purpose
have my
previous
experiences
served in my
development so
far

6)
How will my life
experience
influence and
enhance my
future growth

78- The Transformation Spread

The Transformation Spread is another personal growth evaluator, designed to help you focus more clearly on a specific catalyst for change and the resulting outcome.

The Transformation Spread

Question   Name

                                                    Date

                                                    Time

Feelings or Interpretation   Deck

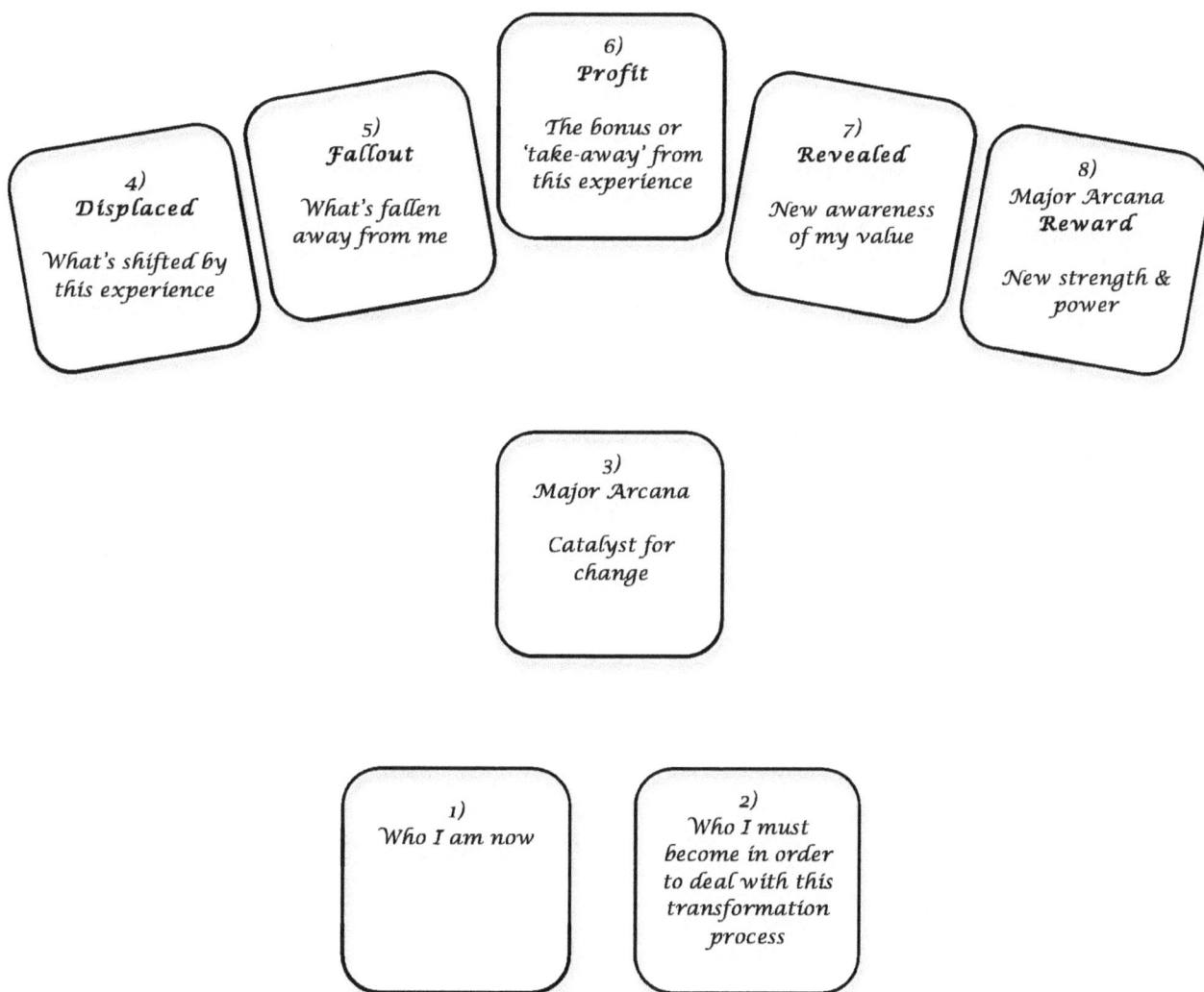

4) **Displaced** — What's shifted by this experience

5) **Fallout** — What's fallen away from me

6) **Profit** — The bonus or 'take-away' from this experience

7) **Revealed** — New awareness of my value

8) Major Arcana **Reward** — New strength & power

3) Major Arcana — Catalyst for change

1) Who I am now

2) Who I must become in order to deal with this transformation process

Created by Sheilaa Hite

79- The New Perspective Spread

The New Perspective Spread provides you with something we can all use to our advantage—a new or different perspective on any given situation.

The New Perspective Spread

Question

Feelings or Interpretation

Name
Date
Time
Deck

6)
Guidance from
the Universe

4)
Internal shift
required

5)
Physical action
required

1)
Question
or
issue

2)
Hidden or
subconscious
perception

3)
Obvious or
conscious
awareness

Created by Sheilaa Hite

80- Super Hero Spread

The **Super Hero Spread** is for all of us 'caped crusaders' who somehow manage to overcome seemingly impossible odds in order to accomplish our goals.

Super Hero Spread

Question

Feelings or Interpretation

Name
Date
Time
Deck

1)

Major Arcana

YOUR
SUPER HERO
SPECIALTY

2)

KRYPTONITE

(Your weak
point)

3)

YOUR MISSION

(Heart of the
matter)

4)

ANTIDOTE TO
KRYPTONITE

(Your strong
point)

5)

Major Arcana

YOUR MENTOR

General Spreads

"It's a step at a time…and these are the steps."
Sheilaa Hite

81- The Temperance Spread

The Temperance Spread is a powerful ally when you're trying to balance several different factors or perspectives in order to get to the best solution. The spread is in the abstract form of a pair of wings.

***If The Temperance card appears in this spread, it will enhance the value of the 'hidden gem' in position #6.

The Temperance Spread

Question

Feelings or Interpretation

Name
Date
Time
Deck

1)
What my heart
tells me

2)
What my head
tells me

7)
Major Arcana

The solution
Divine Guidance
is pointing me
toward

3)
What others
tell me

4)
What I innately
know is true

5)
Where/how do I
balance in order
to shift my
perspective?

6)
Major Arcana

The hidden gem
in this quandary

Inspired by Ciro Marchetti
Created by Sheilaa Hite

82- Gratitude Spread

The **Gratitude Spread** works as a reminder that we can all benefit from consciously acknowledging who, as well as, what we are grateful to.

Gratitude Spread

Question   Name
                                            Date
                                            Time
Feelings or Interpretation   Deck

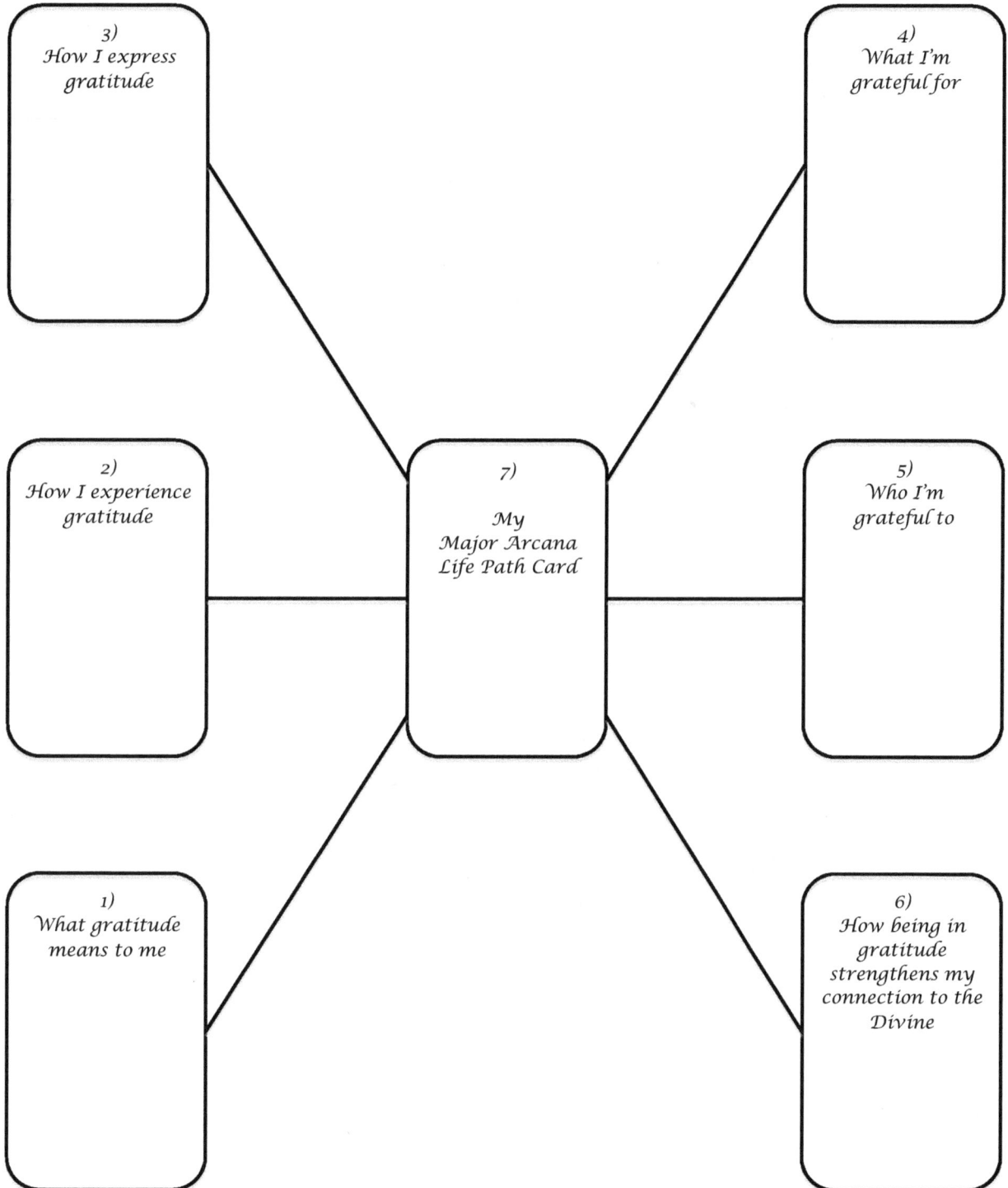

3)
How I express
gratitude

4)
What I'm
grateful for

2)
How I experience
gratitude

7)
My
Major Arcana
Life Path Card

5)
Who I'm
grateful to

1)
What gratitude
means to me

6)
How being in
gratitude
strengthens my
connection to the
Divine

Created by Sheilaa Hite

83- Crossroads

The **Crossroads** spread is perfect for those times when you want more information on your choices and the results or consequences of those choices.

Crossroads

Question

Name
Date
Time

Feelings or Interpretation

Deck

6)
Where this road leads

7)
Where this road leads

4)
What I will encounter if I continue on this road

5)
What I will encounter if I take this different road

3)
Where I am now

1)
Heart of the Matter

2)
What led me here

Created by Linda Farmer
Inspired by Sheilaa Hite

84- New Moon Spread

The **New Moon Spread**. There is an old saying, "What the New Moon promises, the Full Moon brings." Simply put, it means that the events that occur at the time of the New Moon are the seeds that will grow into the results we harvest at the Full Moon. Use this spread to help make your life a wonderful garden!

New Moon Spread

Question   Name
                                            Date
                                            Time
Feelings or Interpretation   Deck

1)
Major Arcana

Where am I
starting from
this month?

2)
What is my
obstacle or
challenge?

3)
Major Arcana

Who/what is my
guide or
inspiration?

7)
Heart of the
matter

4)
What do I need to
release?

6)
Major Arcana

Where am I
headed this
month?

5)
What do I need
to cultivate?

Created by Ginny Guenette

85- The Circus Spread

The Circus Spread. Sometimes the events life presents us with are like the dramatic production that one can only see under the Big Top. Use this spread to figure out where you stand and who the other performers are. It provides solutions to issues, problems or questions that can help you continue to grow.

The Circus Spread

Question

Feelings or Interpretation

Name
Date
Time
Deck

5)
The Spectator

The querent

4)
The Trapeze
Artist

The risks
involved

6)
The Big Top

The probable
outcome

3)
The Bearded
Lady

The unusual or
unexpected

1)
Major Arcana
Ringmaster

The Divine
Intention

7)
Cotton Candy

The gift of the
experience

2)
Flaming Sword
Swallower

The issue or
problem

9)
Major Arcana
The Elephant

The wisdom you
gain as a result

8)
The Clowns

The emotional
banana peel or
pitfalls

86- The Oracle of the Hand Spread

The Oracle of the Hand Spread was inspired by Winslow Eliot's exploration of Palmistry. It's a powerful tool for getting to the essence of any issue and it's one of the most thorough and revealing spreads I've seen.

The Oracle of the Hand Spread

Question

Feelings or Interpretation

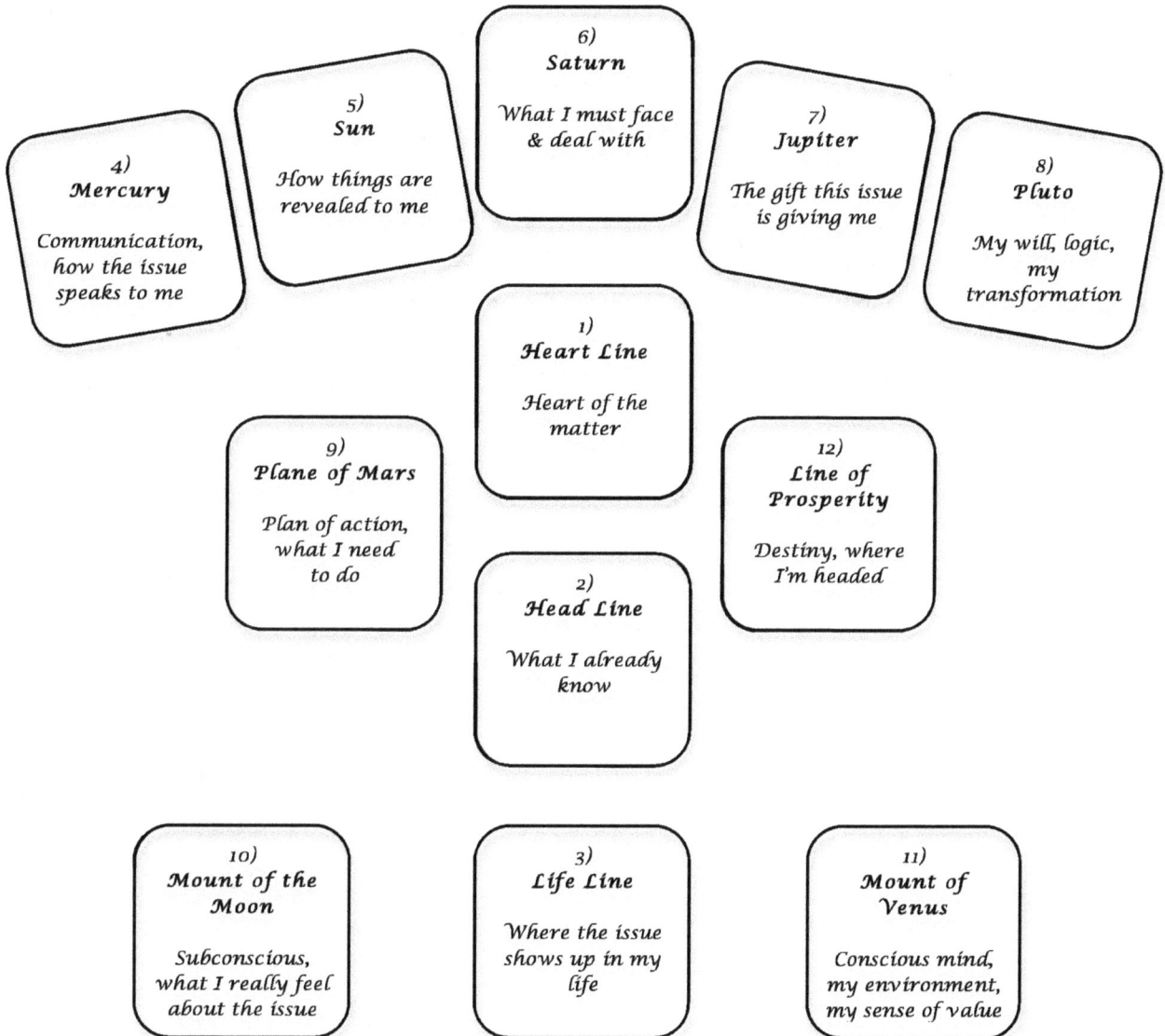

Name

Date

Time

Deck

6)
Saturn

What I must face & deal with

5)
Sun

How things are revealed to me

4)
Mercury

Communication, how the issue speaks to me

7)
Jupiter

The gift this issue is giving me

8)
Pluto

My will, logic, my transformation

1)
Heart Line

Heart of the matter

9)
Plane of Mars

Plan of action, what I need to do

12)
Line of Prosperity

Destiny, where I'm headed

2)
Head Line

What I already know

10)
Mount of the Moon

Subconscious, what I really feel about the issue

3)
Life Line

Where the issue shows up in my life

11)
Mount of Venus

Conscious mind, my environment, my sense of value

87- The Chalice Spread

The Chalice Spread is powerful, informative and really brings out your intuitive abilities. The positions aren't numbered. Think of the 'bowl' part as a container. What does it hold? Think of the 'stem' part as a support. Is it strong or weak? Does it/can it support the 'bowl'?

The Chalice Spread

Question

Feelings or Interpretation

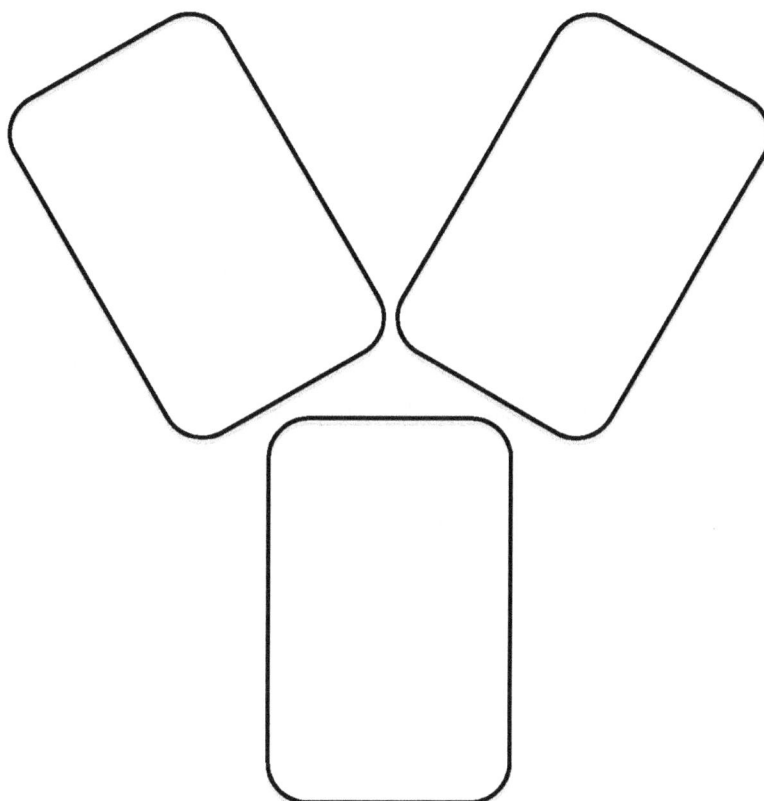

Name
Date
Time
Deck

88- WTF?

The **WTF?** spread answers that question we've all asked at one time or another. It came about when every member of my Tarot Circle Group (myself included) had gone through 'the week from hell.' We needed to know the meaning of each of our experiences and we created this powerful spread that gave us the answers and the solace we were looking for.

WTF?

Question

Name
Date
Time
Deck

Feelings or Interpretation

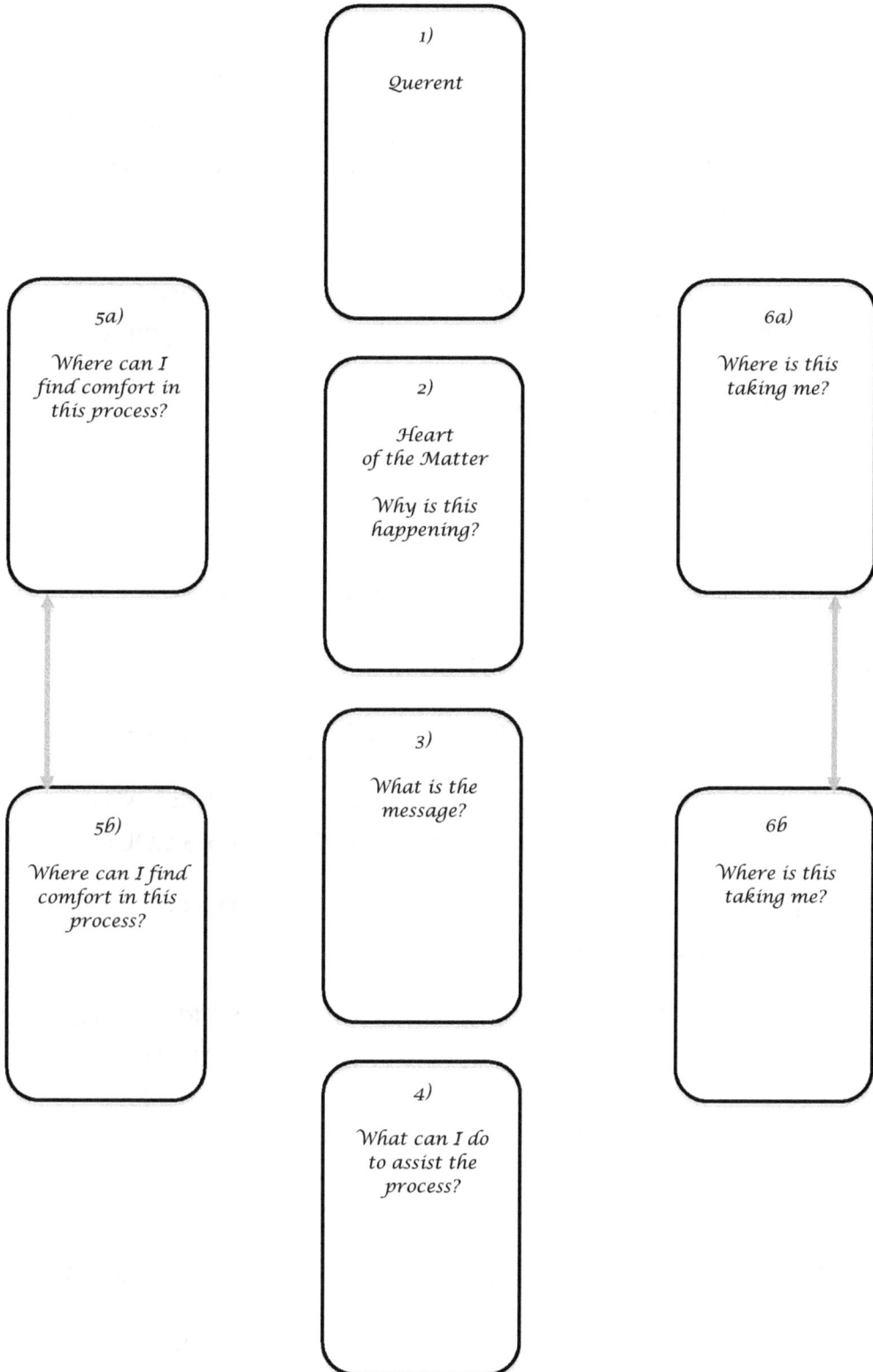

	1) Querent	
5a) Where can I find comfort in this process?	2) Heart of the Matter Why is this happening?	6a) Where is this taking me?
5b) Where can I find comfort in this process?	3) What is the message?	6b Where is this taking me?
	4) What can I do to assist the process?	

Created by Sheilaa Hite's Tarot Circle Group

89- 3 - Card Spread (Linear)

This **3-Card Linear Spread** can be used to answer a variety of questions and to shed light on many different issues. You can "create" this spread any way you want in order to receive the information you're seeking.

Each card represents an aspect of the answer to your question. First, decide which of the ten spreads best relates to your query, and then, moving from left to right, name each position according to the number sequence, i.e., "card 1 represents; card 2 represents; card 3 represents". As you lay the cards out in this order with the appropriate position titles, you will see your answers unfold before you!

* * * Listed here are suggestions to get you started. * * *
Add to the list as you think of other questions and issues you seek answers to

1 - BEGINNING ~ MIDDLE ~ END

2 - NEGATIVE ~ NEUTRAL ~ POSITIVE

3 - BODY ~ MIND ~ SPIRIT

4 - SUBCONSCIOUS ~ CONSCIOUS ~ SUPERCONSCIOUS

5 - OPTION #1 ~ OPTION #2 ~ OPTION #3

6 – WORST CASE SCENARIO ~ NEUTRAL ~ BEST CASE SCENARIO

7 – DISADVANTAGES OF THIS COURSE OF ACTION ~ TRUE NATURE
OF THIS COURSE OF ACTION ~ ADVANTAGES OF THIS COURSE OF ACTION

8 - WHAT IS BEHIND ME (THE PAST) ~ WHERE I STAND NOW (THE PRESENT) ~
WHAT IS BEFORE ME (THE FUTURE)

9 - THE HIDDEN ISSUES IN THIS RELATIONSHIP ~ THE TRUE NATURE OF THIS
RELATIONSHIP ~ WHERE THIS RELATIONSHIP IS HEADED

*** This last 3-card (linear) spread—#10—is excellent for gaining perspective
in any situation by answering the question:*
WHAT'S HAPPENING NOW?

10 -THE NATURE OF THE PRESENT SITUATION ~ MY (or OTHERS) ATTITUDE
TOWARD THIS SITUATION ~ THE MAIN THING TO KEEP IN MIND REGARDING
THIS SITUATION

3 - Card Spread (Linear)

Question   Name
                                                  Date
                                                  Time
Feelings or Interpretation   Deck

1)   2)   3)

90- Is It Worth It?

The **Is It Worth It?** spread helps you determine the potential of an idea, project, situation; if something (or someone) you want is worth the energy and time it'll need to make what you want happen.

Is It Worth It?

Question

Feelings or Interpretation

Name
Date
Time
Deck

3)
What it really is

2)
How the Universe
sees it

4)
Why I want it

6)
The outcome

1)
How I see it

5)
Power I have to
enhance the
potential

91- Empowering Questions Spread

The **Empowering Questions Spread** frees you from the potential pitfall of being overly emotional about an issue, situation or circumstance. It allows you to objectively look at and evaluate the event and yourself.

Empowering Questions Spread

Question   Name
                                                            Date
                                                            Time
Feelings or Interpretation   Deck

1)
What would I do
if I knew
I could not fail?

4)
What is the
most
empowering
thing I can do
now?

7)
What is the
message for me in
this experience?

2)
What is the gift
in this situation?

5)
What is the most
important thing I
can focus on now?

8)
What would I do
if there were
nothing to fear?

3)
What can I learn
from this
experience?

6)
What is the most
supportive thing
I can do now?

Created by Sheilaa Hite

92- Pyramid Spread

The **Pyramid Spread** is a good all-purpose spread. It can be used to answer all kinds of questions and to bring clarity to all types of situations.

Pyramid Spread

Feelings or Interpretation

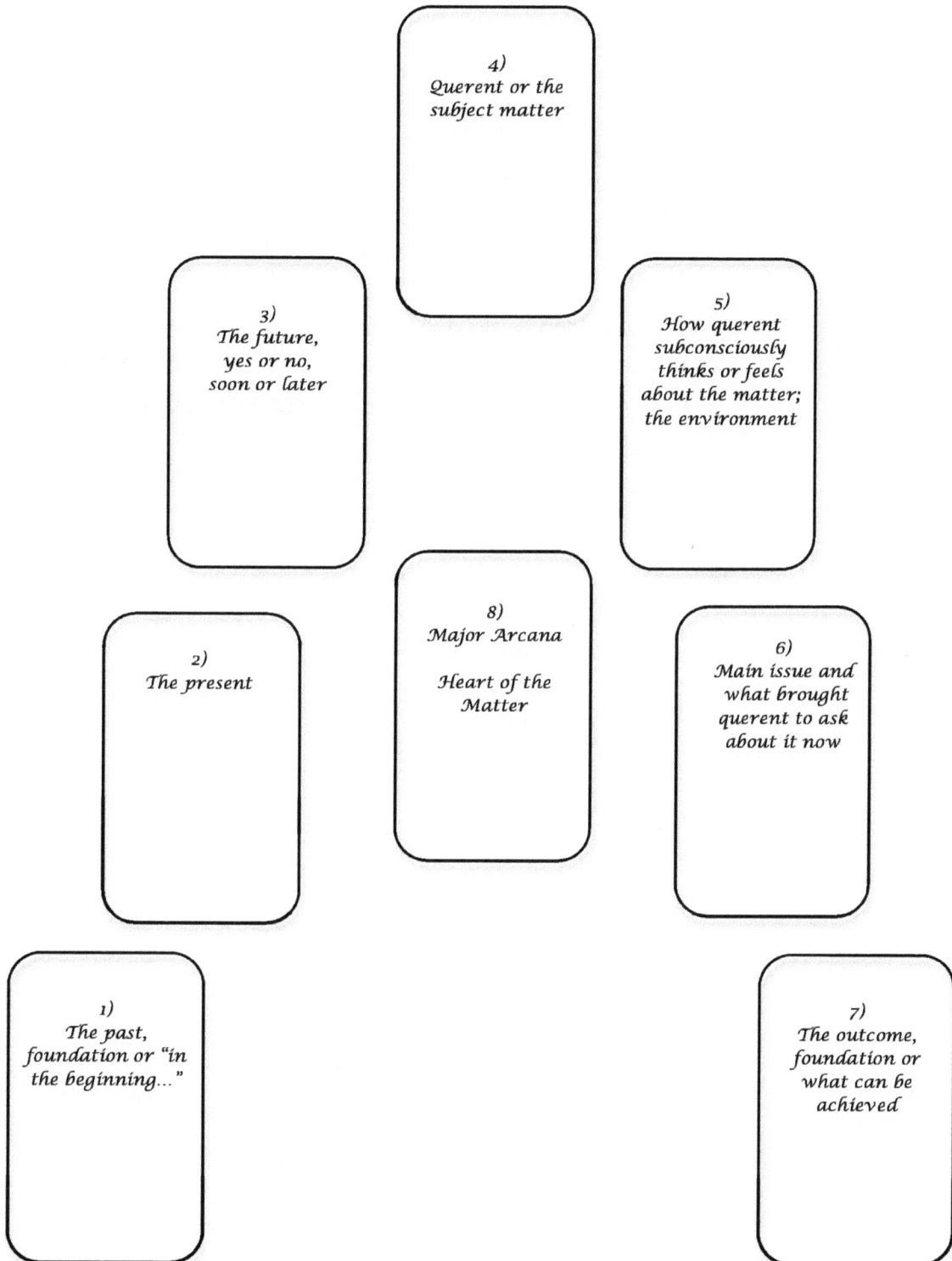

4)
Querent or the
subject matter

3)
The future,
yes or no,
soon or later

5)
How querent
subconsciously
thinks or feels
about the matter;
the environment

8)
Major Arcana

Heart of the
Matter

2)
The present

6)
Main issue and
what brought
querent to ask
about it now

1)
The past,
foundation or "in
the beginning…"

7)
The outcome,
foundation or
what can be
achieved

Created by Sheilaa Hite

93- Healing Heart Meditation

The **Healing Heart Meditation** spread is like a gentle, supportive hug when you're in need of comfort and clarity, especially in times of stress, loss or disappointment. Meditate on each of the cards that appear in the spread and write your experiences in your journal.

Healing Heart Meditation

Question

Name
Date
Time
Deck

Feelings or Interpretation

6)
My ethereal
being

7)
My physical
being

8)
How they (6 & 7)
are meant to
work together

4)
Where/how I am
strong

5)
Where/how I
need support

9)
How Spirit
protects me

2)
What I must
surrender

3)
What I must
embrace

1)
Major Arcana

Guiding message
from Spirit

94- The Process Spread

The Process Spread is the workhorse spread of the group. I use it for almost all of my in-depth questions and issues. It's a truly organic spread, it shows you the stationary and changing dynamics of the situation and the people involved on all levels.

The Process Spread

Question

Feelings or Interpretation

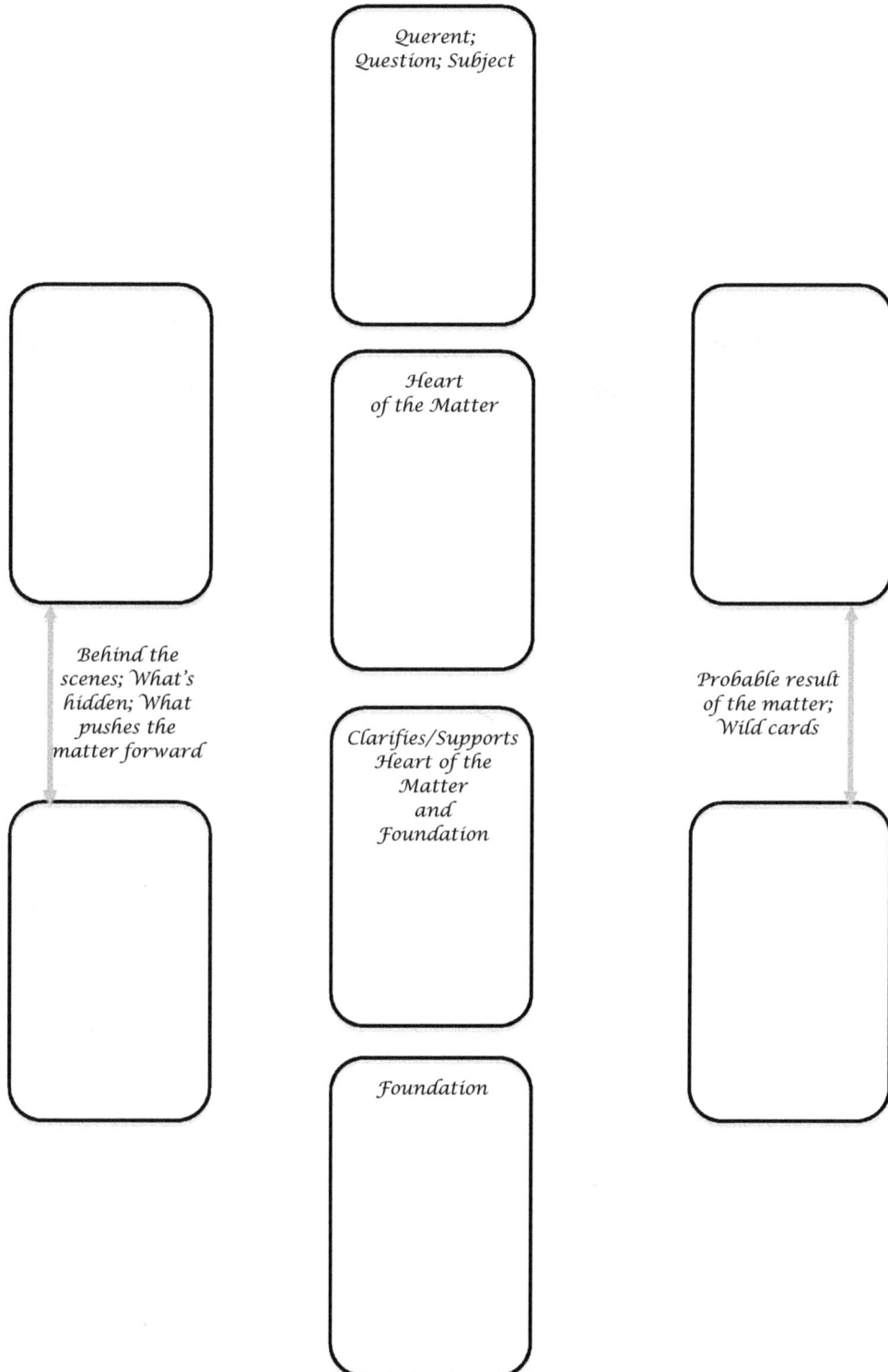

Name
Date
Time
Deck

Querent;
Question; Subject

Heart
of the Matter

Behind the
scenes; What's
hidden; What
pushes the
matter forward

Clarifies/Supports
Heart of the
Matter
and
Foundation

Probable result
of the matter;
Wild cards

Foundation

Created by Sheilaa Hite

95- Flying High

The **Flying High** spread gives you an opportunity to see for yourself how willing you are to let go of limiting circumstances and fly as high as you can in order to bring your visions to fruition.

Flying High

Question   Name
                                                      Date
                                                      Time
Feelings or Interpretation   Deck

┌─────────────────────┐
│ 5)   │
│ Major Arcana   │
│   │
│ What fuels my   │
│ flight?   │
└─────────────────────┘

┌─────────────────────┐
│ 6)   │
│ How high am I   │
│ willing to fly?   │
│   │
│   │
└─────────────────────┘

┌─────────────────────┐
│ 1)   │
│ I am—   │
│   │
│ (choose this   │
│ card face-up)   │
└─────────────────────┘

┌─────────────────────┐
│ 2)   │
│ What limitations   │
│ weigh me down?   │
│   │
│   │
└─────────────────────┘

┌─────────────────────┐
│ 3)   │
│ How have the   │
│ limitations   │
│ served me and I   │
│ them?   │
└─────────────────────┘

┌─────────────────────┐
│ 4)   │
│ What limitations   │
│ am I ready &   │
│ willing to   │
│ release?   │
└─────────────────────┘

Created by Sheilaa Hite

96- Tower Spread

The **Tower Spread** is aptly named because it comes in handy when you are dealing with or need to change. It has a way of showing you important aspects of the issue from subtle, unique perspectives.

Tower Spread

Feelings or Interpretation

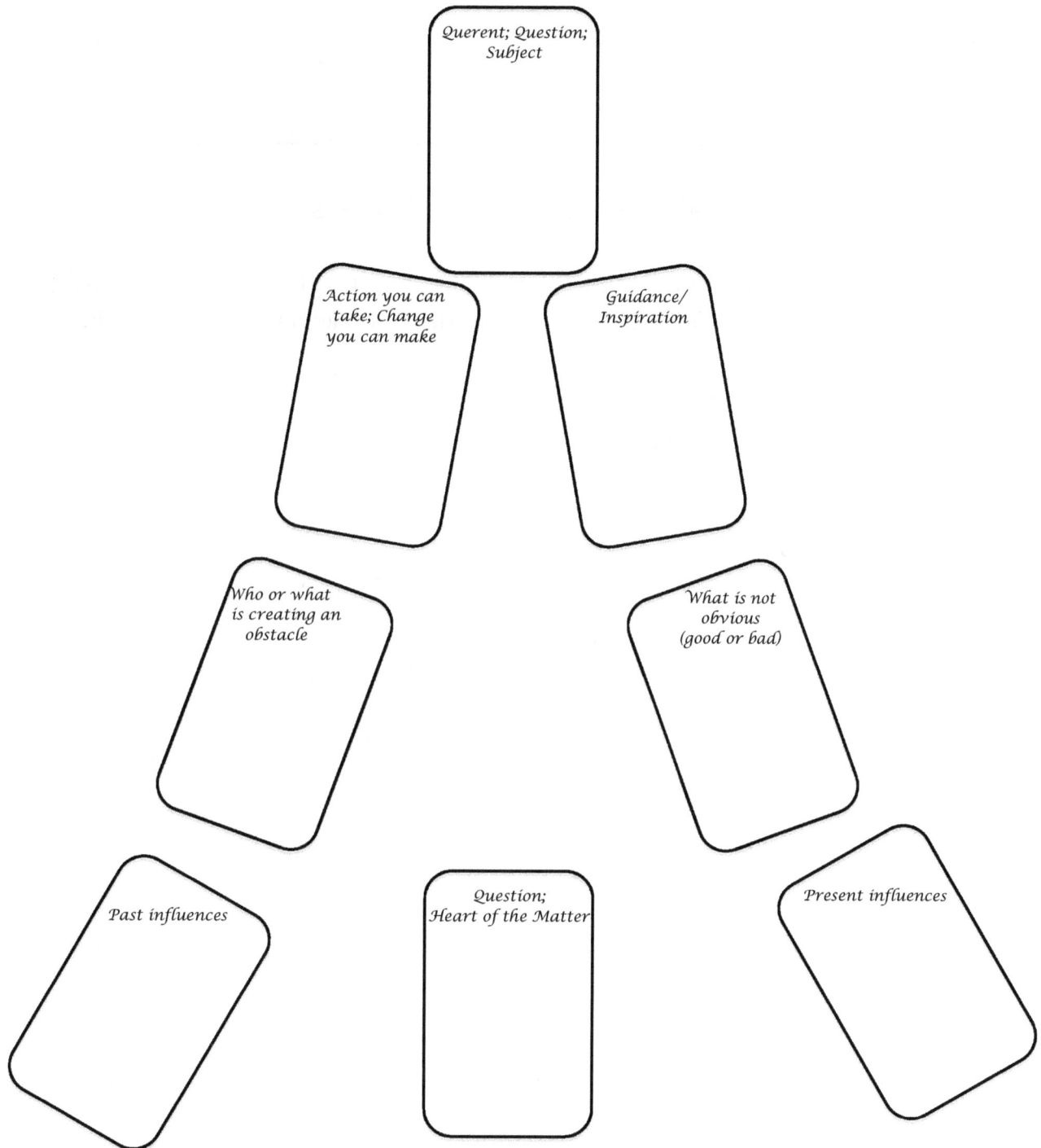

Querent; Question;
Subject

Action you can
take; Change
you can make

Guidance/
Inspiration

Who or what
is creating an
obstacle

What is not
obvious
(good or bad)

Past influences

Question;
Heart of the Matter

Present influences

Created by Sheilaa Hite

97- Message from the Universe

The **Message from the Universe** spread is simple, direct and powerful. It will tell you exactly what the 'Front Office' feels/thinks about whatever question you're asking about.

Message from the Universe

Question

Name
Date
Time
Deck

Feelings or Interpretation

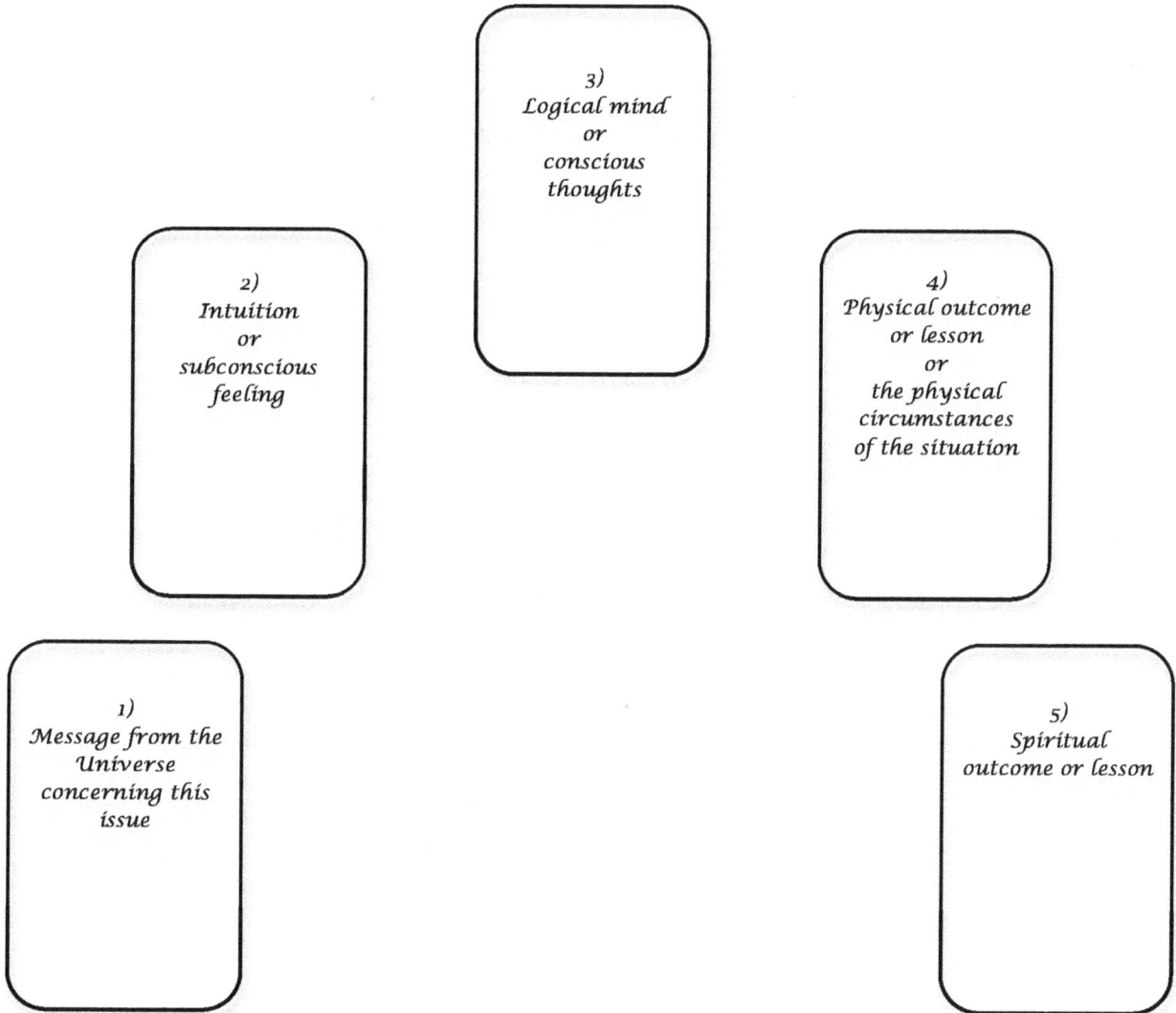

3)
Logical mind
or
conscious
thoughts

2)
Intuition
or
subconscious
feeling

4)
Physical outcome
or lesson
or
the physical
circumstances
of the situation

1)
Message from the
Universe
concerning this
issue

5)
Spiritual
outcome or lesson

Created by David Nathan

98- Dream Interpretation

The **Dream Interpretation** spread will help you decipher the often mysterious clues given to you in your dreams, as well as tell you whether the dream has any validity in your waking life.

Dream Interpretation

Question

Name
Date
Time
Deck

Feelings or Interpretation

3)
What does this dream want me to know?

4)
Why was the message given to me this way?

1)
Major Arcana

Is this a valid message?

5)
What action do I take now?

2)
Is this valid message referring to the material realm?

Created by Sheilaa Hite

99- The Fan Spread

The Fan Spread was inspired by learning that fans have a language all their own. Used properly, the language of the fan will reveal a person's or a situation's true nature in a way that mere words cannot. This spread opens up and reveals the depth of character of the querent, the question and the answer. It gives you an overview of any situation. It's great for identifying limiting old habits so that you can resolve them and move on with a new sense of power and purpose.

The Fan Spread

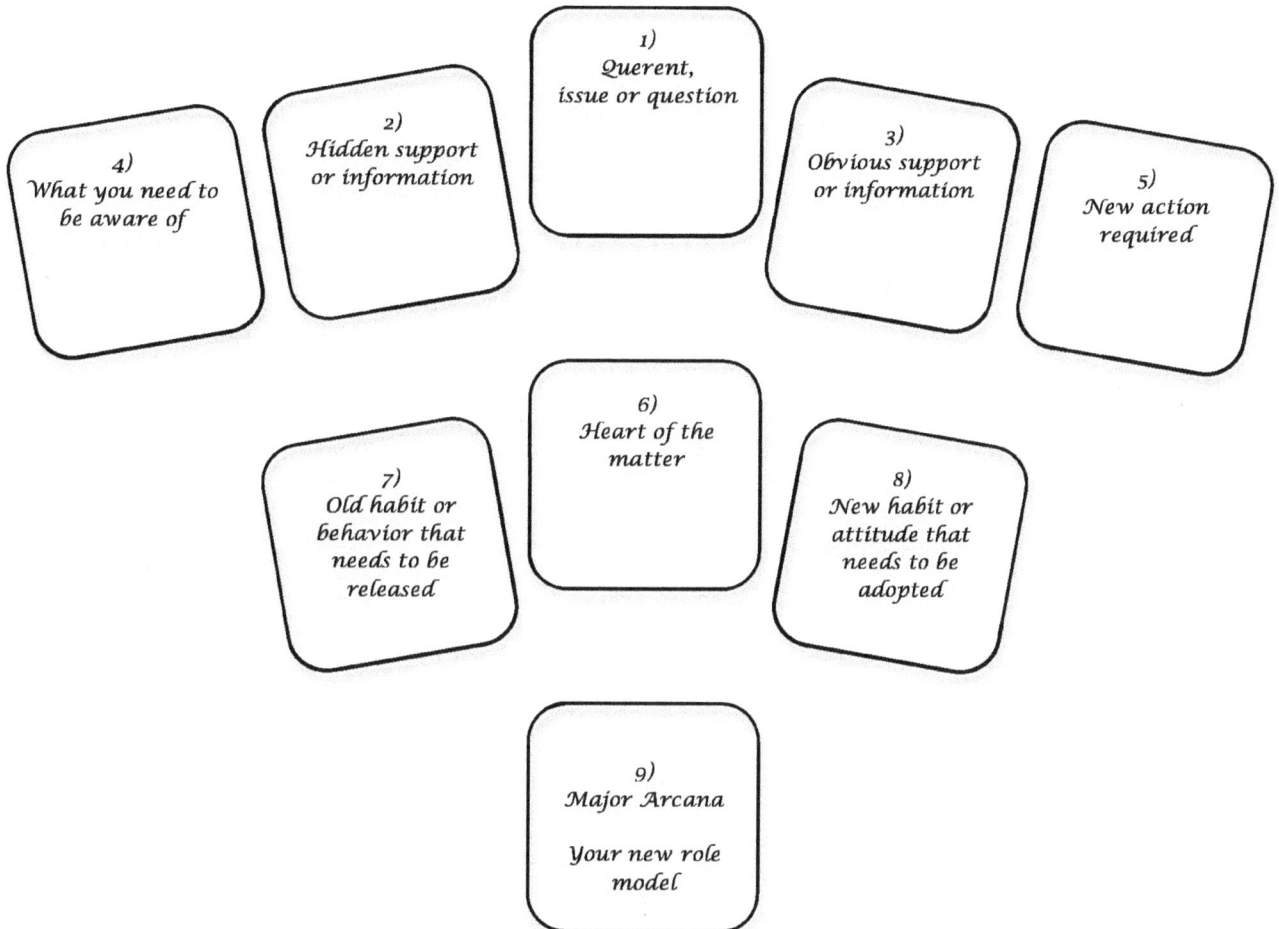

1)
Querent,
issue or question

2)
Hidden support
or information

3)
Obvious support
or information

4)
What you need to
be aware of

5)
New action
required

6)
Heart of the
matter

7)
Old habit or
behavior that
needs to be
released

8)
New habit or
attitude that
needs to be
adopted

9)
Major Arcana

Your new role
model

Created by Sheilaa Hite

100- Ch-Ch-Changes Spread

The **Ch-Ch-Changes Spread** was inspired by a David Bowie song. It's like a good friend who takes you by the hand and walks with you through the often frightening landscape of necessary change. It helps you get clarity on the situation and make the choices necessary for a well-informed transition.

Ch-Ch-Changes Spread

Question

Name
Date
Time
Deck

Feelings or Interpretation

2)
Obvious reason
blocking the
necessary
changes

1)
The situation
that is due for
change

5)
Result Card

How will the
changes
manifest?

3)
Hidden reason
blocking the
necessary
changes

4)
The Bottom Line
& Breakthrough
card

What action
needs to be taken
now

Created by Sheilaa Hite
Inspired by David Bowie

101- Ripples in a Pond

The **Ripples in a Pond** spread is great when you're looking for the answers to questions that deal with the far-reaching effects of a decision or an action.

Ripples in a Pond

Question

Name
Date
Time

Feelings or Interpretation

Deck

4) Subtle or hidden long-term effects/results	3) Hidden from view; Need to be aware of; Energy or action toward or against you	1) Heart of the Matter Querent; Subject matter	2) Environment; Others; Action required; Immediate effects	5) Obvious long-term effects/results

Created by Sheilaa Hite

About the Author

"And those who were seen dancing were thought to be insane by those who could not hear the music."
Angela Monet

Sheilaa Hite, C.Ht., CLC, CPC, is a World Renowned Master Tarot consultant, instructor, Intuitive and author whose ability to expertly interpret and use the power and energy of the Tarot, as well as develop this gift in others, is legendary. Author of the innovative Tarot book, *The Infinite Tarot—The Essential Guide for Connecting to the All-Knowing Source*, she is featured in both editions of Paulette Cooper's book, "The 100 Top Psychics and Astrologers in America."

A naturally gifted Intuitive with an accuracy rate of 95-100%, she was born with the ability to 'see' and interpret information from the ethereal plane far beyond most in her field, bringing practical solutions to both spiritual and worldly issues. Her course—'The Tarot: A Counseling Tool for Psychologists'© makes excellent use of her skills as a teacher-diagnostician and has garnered high praise from the professionals who have consulted with her.

Acknowledged as *"original," "charismatic"* and *"brilliantly insightful"*, she insightfully uses the Tarot, Astrology, Palmistry, Psychometry, Dream and Symbol Interpretation, Mediumship, Channeling, Meditation, Healing and Intuitive Counseling as she helps you understand and fulfill the meaning and purpose of your life. As one of the foremost life-skills mentors alive today, she is also a Certified Clinical Hypnotherapist, Past Life Regressionist, Certified Mentor/Life Coach, Healer, Motivational Speaker and Author.

Although she accepts the title of *'psychic'* (because of the public's limited understanding of the Intuitive Arts), Sheilaa is an *Intuitive* because the power of her abilities stems from her highly developed intuition, which is directly connected to the source of all knowledge—The Creator. Through her powerful connection, she manifests Magic, Miracles and Joy for her clients and herself.

As a media consultant, author and Intuitive, she has been featured on television in such programs as Entertainment Tonight, American Movie Classics, E! Television and NBC's groundbreaking, "The Other Side."

One of only a handful of people in the world permitted by the British government to enter and conduct ceremonies in the sacred 'inner circle of stones' in Stonehenge, she is also the first metaphysician authorized by the city of Malibu, California to teach in their facilities. As a Master of the Sacred Intuitive Arts, she naturally understands the true function of energy and knows how to powerfully work with it to help others influence their successful outcomes.

Her international client list numbers in the thousands and includes TV, movie and sports celebrities, politicians, homemakers, business professionals and members of the clergy and military. Her articles and columns have also appeared on-line, as well as in numerous national and international publications. Through her company, Odysseys—Grand Travel Experiences for the Heart, Spirit, Body and Mind—she also conducts tours and leads retreats to inspiring, beautiful places throughout the world.

As a catalyst of the soul and mind, her extraordinary ability to recognize, integrate and align the energies of the four creative realms have made her mastery at teaching others how to turn "LEAD INTO GOLD" legendary. By synthesizing the expertise of her lifetime, extensive practical experience, sharp business acumen, innate intelligence and spot-on intuition, she uniquely unites and ignites the key elements that help guide her clients and students as they learn the modern-day alchemy secrets of making their dreams come true.

"I love my work, I love that I've been chosen to do it and I love that I'm good at it.
Helping people to be happy and feel empowered makes me happy.
Life is a grand adventure and we are meant to enjoy and grow from the experience."

www.SheilaaHite.com

www.ingramcontent.com/pod-product-compliance
Lightning Source LLC
Chambersburg PA
CBHW080659110426
42739CB00034B/3336